**PRACTICE
MAKES
PERFECT®**

English
Sentence Builder

SECOND EDITION

Ed Swick

Mc
Graw
Hill
Education

New York   Chicago   San Francisco   Athens   London   Madrid
Mexico City   Milan   New Dehli   Singapore   Sydney   Toronto

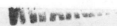

1 2 3 4 5 6 7 8 9   LHS   22 21 20 19 18 17

ISBN   978-1-260-01923-0
MHID   1-260-01923-3

e-ISBN   978-1-260-01924-7
e-MHID   1-260-01924-1

Trademarks: McGraw-Hill Education, the McGraw-Hill Education logo, Practice Makes Perfect, and related trade dress are trademarks or registered trademarks of McGraw-Hill Education and/or its affiliates in the United States and other countries and may not be used without written permission. All other trademarks are the property of their respective owners. McGraw-Hill Education is not associated with any product or vendor mentioned in this book.

Interior design by Village Typographers

McGraw-Hill Education products are available at special quantity discounts to use as premiums and sales promotions or for use in corporate training programs. To contact a representative, please visit the Contact Us pages at www.mhprofessional.com.

Contents

Introduction

Writing skills are usually the most difficult skills to acquire in a language. This is particularly true in a foreign language. The goal of this book is to reduce that difficulty as it guides you through the various types of structures in the English language and illustrates how those structures combine to make sentences.

Naturally, in order to acquire writing skills you have *to write*. Therefore, you will be provided with an abundance of writing exercises. Some will require a small variation in a given sentence. Others will provide you with a series of words that you form into an appropriate sentence. And you will have plenty of opportunity for coming up with original sentences of your own. This development of writing better English sentences moves gradually and with careful explanation from the least complex activity to the most complex.

Make changes to given sentences.
Combine a series of words as a sentence. } Writing skills developed
Write original sentences.

In addition to the illustrations of how structures combine to form sentences and to the exercises for practice, an Answer Key is provided at the end of the book. It includes not only the correct answers for the exercises but also sample sentences, with which you can compare your original sentences. The final chapter, Chapter 21, is a *Progress Check*, which can help you determine what areas of structure you might want to review in order to improve how you use certain grammatical concepts.

Good sentence writing is not an impossible task, but it requires analysis and practice and a willingness to apply concepts and rules consistently. Let this book guide you, and you will discover a new confidence for writing more successfully in English.

Have fun and write well!

Declarative sentences and word order

Declarative sentences in English consist of a subject and predicate. The verb in the predicate is conjugated appropriately for the subject and in a specific tense:

subject + predicate

Mary + speaks English.

Let's look at some examples that illustrate this. Declarative sentences can have a singular or plural noun as their subject and can be followed by a verb in any tense and by the complement of the sentence.

John repairs the car.
The boys ran into the forest.

Other declarative sentences use a pronoun as their subject, and again the tense of the sentence can vary.

She has never been to England.	*singular-pronoun subject, present-perfect-tense verb*
We shall visit them soon.	*plural-pronoun subject, future-tense verb*

Since English verbs can show an incomplete action or one in progress (**he is going**) or a completed or habitual action (**he goes**), when changing tenses, you have to conform to the type of action of the verb. For example:

he is going, he was going, he has been going
he goes, he went, he has gone

The conjugation of English verbs is, with few exceptions, a relatively simple matter, but using the proper tenses of verbs is something else. It is particularly important to understand the tense differences between verbs that describe an action in progress and verbs that describe a completed or habitual action.

Incomplete actions

Let's look at some sentences that illustrate the meaning of incomplete actions—or ones in progress—in the present, past, and future tenses. Note that in some cases, it is an *interruption* of some kind that causes the action to be incomplete. (To the right of the examples are italicized clarifications that will help you fully understand the example sentences.)

1

Present tense

He **is washing** the car.

He has not finished. The car still has some dirty spots.

We **are building** a tree house.

The tree house is not yet finished.

Past tense

I **was sleeping** when he called.

I didn't finish my nap. His call interrupted my sleep.

The men **were working** in the mine but suddenly quit.

The work in the mine is unfinished, because the men quit.

Future tense

He **will be playing** in a rock band.

There is no apparent end to his job in the band.

Sarah **will be needing** more money.

There is no apparent end to Sarah's need for money.

Completed actions

Compare those examples with the following sentences that illustrate verbs that describe completed or habitual actions:

Present tense

He **washes** the car every Sunday.

His habit is to wash the car on Sunday.

They **live** in the capital.

Their regular place of residence is the capital.

Past tense

The puppy **slept** with me every night.

The puppy's habit was to sleep with me.

I **worked** in Mexico for five years.

My work for five years was in Mexico. I work elsewhere now.

Future tense

He **will play** a hymn for us on the piano.

He is going to play the hymn just once.

Uncle Bill **will arrive** today.

Uncle Bill will arrive today only once.

The perfect tenses conform to the same kinds of meanings. For example:

Incomplete action or one in progress

He **has been washing** the car for three hours.
I **had been sleeping** in the den.
The men **will have been working** on it for twenty-four hours by tomorrow.

Completed or habitual action

They **have lived** here since June.
The pup **had never slept** so long before.
Uncle Bill **will have arrived** home by the time we get there.

Rewrite the following declarative sentences in the missing tenses.

1. a. Present _____

    Past <u>Thomas found the wallet.</u>

    b. Present perfect _____

    c. Past perfect _____

    d. Future _____

2 Present <u>The men are trying to raze the barn.</u>

    a. Past _____

    b. Present perfect _____

    c. Past perfect _____

    d. Future _____

3. a. Present _____

    b. Past _____

    c. Present perfect _____

    d. Past perfect _____

    Future <u>They will drop by at two P.M.</u>

4. a. Present _____

    b. Past _____

    Present perfect <u>She has been working here as a counselor.</u>

    c. Past perfect _____

    d. Future _____

5. Present <u>I have no time.</u>

    a. Past _____

    b. Present perfect _____

    c. Past perfect _____

    d. Future _____

6. a. Present _____

    b. Past _____

    c. Present perfect _____

    Past perfect <u>The wealthy couple had traveled the world on their yacht.</u>

    d. Future _____

Change the following sentences from actions in progress to completed or habitual actions. Add or remove words as needed to make sense. Keep the same tense as the original sentence.

EXAMPLE: Bill is still eating his breakfast.

<u>Bill eats his breakfast at seven thirty A.M.</u>

1. The attorneys were drawing up the contracts for the merger.

   _____

2. I will probably still be cooking when you arrive.

   _____

3. The boys will be sleeping in the little room in the attic.

   _____

4. I have been hoping for a long time to have a visit from you.

   _____

5. They had been sitting on the porch when the storm came up.

   _____

Follow the same directions, but change from completed or habitual actions to actions in progress.

6. We shall work even harder.

   _____

7. They traveled to Greece this year.

   _____

8. She cried when he left.

   _____

9. Bill and I often play catch in the backyard.

   _____

10. I hope the two boys will finally pass the test.

    _____

Recognizing tense from context

With certain verbs, it is the context of the sentence that tells you which tense is implied, because these verbs are identical, except for the third-person singular, in both the present and past tenses. Six such verbs are **cut**, **put**, **let**, **set**, **quit**, and **read**. Let's look at one of these verbs (**cut**) and how it is conjugated in the present and past tenses.

| Present | I cut, you cut, he cuts, we cut, you cut, they cut |
| Past | I cut, you cut, he cut, we cut, you cut, they cut |

As you can clearly see, it is only in the third-person-singular present tense (**he cuts**) where there is any difference between the present-tense and past-tense conjugations. Therefore, in order to know which tense is being used in a sentence, you must consider the context of the sentence. (Naturally, in the case of the verb **read**, there is a difference in the pronunciation of the two tenses. It is in their written form where the distinction must be made.)

Certain adverbs act as signals that tell whether these verbs are being used in the present or past tense, adverbs such as **today**, **yesterday**, and **tomorrow**. Remember that an English present tense can indicate the future tense; therefore, **tomorrow** is an appropriate signal for distinguishing the tense of these verbs. For example:

Present	He **quits** working here **today**.
Past	He **quit yesterday** after only five days on the job.
Future	He **quits tomorrow** after more than thirty years with us.

Let's look at some examples, in which the subject is not a third-person singular. Also keep in mind that other adverbial phrases and expressions can indicate the past or the future; for example: **last year** or **next week**. Other verbs in a sentence also signal the tense.

Present-tense verb as a tense signal

You **are** careless and always let the dog run away.
I **get** the dishes and set the table.
I **find** the right paragraph and read in a loud voice.

Past-tense verb or adverbial expression as a tense signal

He quit school **when still a teenager**.
The bread is stale because I cut it **two days ago**.
She **opened** the book and put on her glasses.

When these verbs describe an action in progress or are used with an auxiliary, there is no difficulty in determining the tense of the sentence. For example:

They **were reading** the newspaper.	*past*
The sun **is setting**.	*present*
I **won't let** this happen again!	*future*

Exercise
1·3

In the space provided, write the tense of the sentence: present, past, or future.

1. _____ She lets me borrow her notebook.

2. _____ I read that novel back in high school.

3. _____ The toddler cut his finger again.

4. _____ The explorers set out on another journey last month.

5. _____ She was putting on her dress when she fell.

6. _____ My brother quits a new job every few weeks.

7. _____ No one read the article.

8. _____ The judge put the thief in jail again.

9. _____ Tomorrow I quit for sure!

10. _____ We won't set foot in this restaurant ever again!

There are several other verbs that are identical in the present and past tenses. They are as follows:

beat	hit	split
bet	hurt	spread
burst	rid	thrust
cast	slit	wet
cost	shed	

The tense of these verbs is determined by usage and certain signals included in a sentence. For example:

Present: Those houses cost more than they did a month ago.
Past: It hurt for about an hour, but it feels a lot better now.
Future: Tomorrow morning we hit the road for home.

Types of complements

The complement of a declarative sentence can be an adjective, an adverb, a prepositional phrase, an object, or a combination of these elements.

subject + predicate + adjective/adverb/prepositional phrase/object

Consider these examples with an adjective and an adverb:

The children were **noisy**.	*adjective*
His eyes blinked **rapidly**.	*adverb*

The following examples illustrate a prepositional phrase and a direct object:

Our relatives sat **in the garden**.	*prepositional phrase*
I don't know **Mr. Walker**.	*direct object*

The following example illustrates a combination of those elements.

They approached **the house cautiously from the rear**.	*combination of elements*

Exercise
1·4

Using the verbs provided as cues, write original sentences in the tenses specified.

EXAMPLE: buy / present habitual

He buys something new every day.

1. apply / present completed or habitual

_____

2. suggest / present in progress or incomplete

_____

3. annoy / present perfect in progress or incomplete

_____

4. remain / future completed or habitual

_____

5. attempt / past in progress or incomplete

_____

6. trick / present perfect completed or habitual

_____

7. rub / past completed or habitual

_____

8. earn / future in progress or incomplete

_____

9. harvest / past perfect completed or habitual

_____

10. lend / present perfect in progress or incomplete

_____

Exercise 1·5

Complete the following sentences twice with the type of complement specified.

EXAMPLE: adverb or adverbial phrase

The men had to work <u>slowly</u>.

The men had to work <u>every day</u>.

1. adverb or adverbial phrase

   a. Tina wrote him _____

   b. Tina wrote him _____

2. prepositional phrase

   a. James chatted _____

   b. James chatted _____

3. direct object

   a. Dad wanted to sell _____

   b. Dad wanted to sell _____

4. direct and indirect object

   a. Bob sent _____

   b. Bob sent _____

5. adjective

   a. She was always _____

   b. She was always _____

6. combination of elements

   a. Mary drove _____

   b. Mary drove _____

7. adverb or adverbial phrase

   a. She was practicing _____

   b. She was practicing _____

8. prepositional phrase

   a. I met him _____

   b. I met him _____

9. direct and indirect object

   a. I will give _____

   b. I will give _____

10. combination of elements

   a. The soldiers ran _____

   b. The soldiers ran _____

Placing emphasized elements first

In order to emphasize a specific element (such as an adverb or prepositional phrase) in a declarative sentence, it is possible to place that element ahead of the subject. The positions of the other elements of the sentence (subject, verb, predicate) do not change.

     emphasized element + subject + predicate + complement

Emphasized elements tend to tell *when* or *how often* something is done (**usually, ordinarily, in the winter, today, during summer vacation**). For example:

They went to a concert yesterday.	=	Yesterday they went to a concert.
He brushes his teeth every morning.	=	Every morning he brushes his teeth.
The girls play chess in the evening.	=	In the evening the girls play chess.

If a long prepositional phrase is the first element of a sentence, it is common to separate it from the rest of the sentence by a comma. For example:

> Without looking back at his parents, John quickened his pace and turned the corner.
> After hearing the good news, Mary embraced Bill and kissed him.
> Although Johnny was a rather short boy, he was chosen as captain of the basketball team.

Commas can also be used to separate a highly emphasized adverb from the rest of the sentence:

> Truthfully, I really never saw the accident happen.

Exercise 1·6

Begin each sentence that follows with four different adverbs or prepositional phrases.

EXAMPLE: <u>Today</u> she finally felt well again.

<u>After a long illness</u>, she finally felt well again.

<u>Incredibly</u>, she finally felt well again.

<u>Happily</u>, she finally felt well again.

1. a. _____ Granddad arrived soaking wet.

   b. _____ Granddad arrived soaking wet.

   c. _____ Granddad arrived soaking wet.

   d. _____ Granddad arrived soaking wet.

2. a. _____ I spent too much money.

   b. _____ I spent too much money.

   c. _____ I spent too much money.

   d. _____ I spent too much money.

3. a. _____ his son had learned a serious lesson.

   b. _____ his son had learned a serious lesson.

   c. _____ his son had learned a serious lesson.

   d. _____ his son had learned a serious lesson.

4. a. _____ we will go sightseeing in Madrid.

   b. _____ we will go sightseeing in Madrid.

   c. _____ we will go sightseeing in Madrid.

   d. _____ we will go sightseeing in Madrid.

5. a. _____ their village was completely destroyed.

   b. _____ their village was completely destroyed.

   c. _____ their village was completely destroyed.

   d. _____ their village was completely destroyed.

6. a. _____ he finally grew to like the new house and neighborhood.

   b. _____ he finally grew to like the new house and neighborhood.

   c. _____ he finally grew to like the new house and neighborhood.

   d. _____ he finally grew to like the new house and neighborhood.

Using negatives

Declarative sentences do not have to make positive statements. They can be negated by using any of a variety of negative words: **no**, **not**, **not any**, **none**, **nothing**, **no one**, **never**, **nowhere**, or **nobody**. Let's look at an example with each of these negative words:

> I have **no** time for this now.
> You are **not** allowed to smoke here.
> She does **not** want **any** contact with you.
> **None** of the contestants knew the answer.
> I have **nothing** more to say to you.
> He spoke to **no one** about it.
> They **never** really expected to win the lottery.
> There's **nowhere** I'd rather live than right here.
> **Nobody** saw the burglar enter the house.

Except with the verb **to be**, a form of **do** is used when negating a verb with **not**. The object of the verb will be preceded by a form of **any**. If a form of **no** is used as the negative, **do** is not required. Compare the following sentences:

I want **no** money from you.	=	I **don't** want any money from you.
Tom has **no** time.	=	Tom **does not** have any time.
There is **no** one here to help me.	=	There **isn't** anyone here to help me.

The forms of **no** and **any** are as follows:

no	not any
no one	not anyone
nobody	not anybody
nowhere	not anywhere
nothing	not anything

A form of **no** or a form of **not any** can be used to replace one another.

a form of *no* = a form of *do not* + a form of *any*

I have **no** money.	=	I **do not** have **any** money.

A form of **do** is used only with the negation of verbs in the present and past tenses. With modal auxiliaries or auxiliaries of the perfect and future tenses, avoid **do**.

She **could do no** better.	=	She **couldn't do** any better.
The boy **has caused no** problems.	=	The boy **hasn't caused** any problems.
Mr. Cole **will accept no** excuses.	=	Mr. Cole **won't accept** any excuses.

auxiliary with a form of *no* = auxiliary with *not* + a form of *any*

I **will buy no** gifts.	=	I **will not buy any** gifts.

*Rewrite each sentence with a form of **not any**. Retain the tense of the original sentence.*

EXAMPLE: The teacher found no errors.

The teacher didn't find any errors.

1. John could take no one's advice.

   _____

2. I will accept nothing but excellence.

   _____

3. There is nowhere for you to hide.

   _____

4. Ms. Brooks spoke with nobody about the problem.

   _____

5. You should give no one so young that kind of responsibility.

   _____

6. That will take no time at all.

   _____

7. There was none left for the little children.

   _____

8. There was no one for him to turn to.

   _____

9. My parents had found no place to spend the night.

   _____

10. They will achieve nothing from their efforts.

   _____

2

Interrogative sentences

There are two types of interrogative sentences, and both types ask questions. The first type can be called a **yes-no** question, because the answer to such a question will begin with the affirmative word **yes** or the negative word **no**. Most questions of this type begin with a form of the auxiliary verb **do**.

> **auxiliary + subject + verb + predicate +?**

> Do + you + have + the books +?

Yes-no questions

If the verb in a **yes-no** question is the verb **to be** or the verb **to have**, the question is formed simply by placing the verb before the subject of the sentence.

> **to be/to have + subject + predicate +?**

> Is + she + the new student +?

This occurs in any tense. In the case of the perfect tenses or the future tense, it is the auxiliary of the verbs **to be** and **to have** that precede the subject. For example:

Present	**Is** she aware of the problem?
Past	**Was** there enough time to finish the exam?
Present perfect	**Have** you been here before?
Future	**Will** Professor Burns be today's lecturer again?
Present	**Have** you enough money for the tickets?
Past	**Had** he adequate notice?
Present perfect	**Has** your mother had the operation yet?
Future	**Will** the workers have some time off?

Auxiliaries

This kind of question structure, in which the verb precedes the subject, also occurs with numerous auxiliaries, such as the following:

be able to	ought to
can	shall/will
could	should
have	would
must	

auxiliary + subject + verb form + predicate +?

Should + we + help + them +?

Let's look at some example sentences:

Are you **able to** make out her signature?
Have you worked here for very long?
Ought she **to** have said that to her mother?

Notice in each example that the sentence contains a second verb. The initial verb is an auxiliary, and it is followed by an infinitive (such as **to work**) or by an elliptical infinitive, which omits the particle word (**to**); for example: **are you able to make**, **will you try**. With most auxiliaries, it is the tense of the auxiliary that determines the "time" of the action; for example: present (**can he speak**) and past (**could he speak**).

With the auxiliary **have**, however, its tense conjugation combined with a past participle (and not an infinitive) identifies the tense as either present perfect, past perfect, or future perfect:

Present perfect	has he spoken
Past perfect	had he spoken
Future perfect	will he have spoken

The auxiliaries **shall** and **will** identify the future tense and are followed by elliptical infinitives:

Shall I get you something for dinner?
Will you be staying the night?

In declarative sentences, most English speakers use **will**, although technically, **shall** should be used with singular and plural pronouns in the first person, and **will** should be used with the second and third persons. In questions, the rule is applied more strictly: **shall** with first-person singular and plural, and **will** with second- and third-persons singular and plural.

	Singular	Plural
First	**Shall** I turn on the TV?	**Shall** we go to the movies tonight?
Second	Tom, **will** you help me with this?	Boys, **will** you please stop your arguing?
Third	**Will** she like this dress?	**Will** they be able to spend some time with us?

It is important to be knowledgeable about the other auxiliaries and how they function in the various tenses. Let's focus on two that can be conjugated like other verbs and form questions by placing the conjugated verb or its auxiliaries before the subject:

Present	**Is** she able to stand alone?
Past	**Was** she able to stand alone?
Present perfect	**Has** she been able to stand alone?
Future	**Will** she be able to stand alone?
Present	**Have** you a few extra dollars?
Past	**Had** you a few extra dollars?
Present perfect	**Have** you had a few extra dollars?
Future	**Will** you have a few extra dollars?

Compare **to be able to** and **have** with the following auxiliaries and what occurs with them in the various tenses:

- ◆ **Can** changes to **to be able to**

Present	**Can** Victor understand the problem?
Past	**Could** Victor understand the problem?
Present perfect	Has Victor **been able to** understand the problem?
Future	Will Victor **be able to** understand the problem?

- ◆ **Ought to** changes to **ought to have**

Present	**Ought** you to speak so harshly?
Past	*Ought to is not used in a past-tense question.*
Present perfect	**Ought** you **to have** spoken so harshly?
Future	*Ought to is not used in a future-tense question.*

- ◆ **Must** changes to **have to**

Present	**Must** he live alone?
Past	Did he **have to** live alone?
Present perfect	Has he **had to** live alone?
Future	Will he **have to** live alone?

- ◆ **Should** changes to **should have**

Present	**Should** they argue so much?
Past	*Should is not used in a past-tense question.*
Present perfect	**Should** they **have** argued so much?
Future	*Should is not used in a future-tense question.*

Questions with *do/did*

Verbs that are not auxiliaries form questions by beginning them in the present tense with **do** and in the past tense with **did**. The use of **do/did** does not occur in the other tenses. Let's examine a few cases in point:

Present	**Do** you enjoy her classes?
Past	**Did** you enjoy her classes?
Present perfect	Have you enjoyed her classes?
Future	Will you enjoy her classes?

Present	**Does** Thomas visit you often?
Past	**Did** Thomas visit you often?
Present perfect	Has Thomas visited you often?
Future	Will Thomas visit you often?

Since **have** is an auxiliary, it can be used in questions without **do/did**. Nevertheless, there is a tendency to add the extra **do/did** auxiliary both in speech and in writing.

Present	**Do** you have a few extra dollars?
Past	**Did** you have a few extra dollars?
Present perfect	Have you had a few extra dollars?
Future	Will you have a few extra dollars?

When using **have to** (which is much the same as **must** in meaning), you must use **do/did** in the present and past tenses.

Present	**Do** they have to work so many hours?
Past	**Did** they have to work so many hours?
Present perfect	Have they had to work so many hours?
Future	Will they have to work so many hours?

The auxiliaries **to want to** and **to like to** form their present- and past-tense questions with **do/did**. For example:

Present	**Does** Mom want to go shopping?
Past	**Did** Mom want to go shopping?
Present perfect	Has Mom wanted to go shopping?
Future	Will Mom want to go shopping?

Present	**Do** they like to listen to rap music?
Past	**Did** they like to listen to rap music?
Present perfect	Have they liked to listen to rap music?
Future	Will they like to listen to rap music?

You should be aware that while both **to want to** and **to like to** are auxiliary verbs, they are also used as transitive verbs, taking a direct object. When they are used as transitive verbs, the final **to** is omitted from the verb: **to want** and **to like**. Even when used as transitive verbs, they form their present- and past-tense questions with **do/did**.

do/did + subject + *want/like* + predicate +?

Does + she + like + him +?

Present	**Do** you want some help?
	Does she like pizza?
Past	**Did** you want some help?
	Did she like pizza?

Exercise

2·1

Rewrite the following questions in the missing tenses.

1. a. Present _____

   b. Past _____

   c. Present perfect _____

      Future Will you be home for the holidays?

2. a. Present _____

      Past Did the arsonist burn down the bank?

   b. Present perfect _____

   c. Future _____

3. a. Present _____

   b. Past _____

      Present perfect Have you had to spend a lot of time studying?

   c. Future _____

4. a. Present _____

   b. Past _____

   Present perfect <u>Have the workers done the job right?</u>

   c. Future _____

5. Present <u>Can you really predict the outcome of the election?</u>

   a. Past _____

   b. Present perfect _____

   c. Future _____

Exercise
2·2

Write original questions with the following auxiliaries in the tense shown in parentheses.

EXAMPLE: can (past) <u>Could you see over the tall hedge?</u>

1. should (present perfect) _____

2. must (present) _____

3. want to (future) _____

4. have to (present) _____

5. have (future) _____

6. be able to (present) _____

7. will (future) _____

8. ought to (present perfect) _____

9. would (present) _____

10. must (present perfect) _____

Exercise
2·3

*Using the phrases provided, first form a **yes-no** question. Then change the question by adding any appropriate auxiliary.*

EXAMPLE: to walk to work

<u>Do you always walk to work?</u>

<u>Do you always have to walk to work?</u>

1. to spend more than a hundred dollars

   a. _____

   b. _____

2. to arrive in the capital on time

   a. _____

   b. _____

3. to develop a new method

   a. _____

   b. _____

4. to remain calm

   a. _____

   b. _____

5. to consider the danger

   a. _____

   b. _____

6. to spell accurately

   a. _____

   b. _____

7. to prepare some lunch

   a. _____

   b. _____

8. to suggest a solution

   a. _____

   b. _____

9. to flee the storm

   a. _____

   b. _____

10. to pretend nothing is wrong

   a. _____

   b. _____

Progressive-form questions

Just as in a declarative sentence, verbs in a question can be formed in the progressive, which means that they are actions in progress or incomplete. Since the progressive form is composed of a conjugation of **to be** plus a present participle (**is going**, **was singing**), and **to be** never forms a question with **do/did**, all questions that have a progressive verb will begin with the verb **to be** or its auxiliaries.

> **to be** + subject + present participle (-ing) +?

> **Are** + you + working in the garden +?

For example:

Present	**Are** you planning on attending the party?
Past	**Was** she sleeping when the storm hit?
Present perfect	**Have** the men been working in the mine again?
Future	**Will** he be preparing for final exams?

Be aware that a verb in a **do/did** question will not require the auxiliary **do/did** when it is changed to its progressive form. For example:

Do you attend a state university?
Are you attending a state university?

Did the campers sleep in tents?
Were the campers sleeping in tents?

Exercise
2·4

Change each of the following sentences to a question. Then, in a second question, change the verb to the progressive form. Be sure to retain the tense of the original sentence.

EXAMPLE:　　Bill learned shorthand.

Did Bill learn shorthand?

Was Bill learning shorthand?

1. A plumber fixed the leaking pipes.

   a. _____

   b. _____

2. You couldn't work on that old car.

   a. _____

   b. _____

3. The judges have spoken about this for a long time.

   a. _____

   b. _____

4. Time goes by very fast.

    a. _____

    b. _____

5. Thunder rolled across the foothills.

    a. _____

    b. _____

6. You will take a series of exams.

    a. _____

    b. _____

7. Mr. Kelly has wanted to vacation there.

    a. _____

    b. _____

8. He's crazy.

    a. _____

    b. _____

9. The revelers have had a good time at the celebration.

    a. _____

    b. _____

10. I should sit nearer to her.

    a. _____

    b. _____

Questions using interrogative words

The second kind of question formation is one that begins with an interrogative word: **who**, **what**, **why**, **how**, **which**, or **when**. The rules that appy about the use of **do/did** in questions apply in the same way with questions that begin with an interrogative word. For example:

Can he understand you?	**How** can he understand you?
Do you like that man?	**Why** do you like that man?
Are you coming to the party?	**When** are you coming to the party?
Have you found the books?	**Where** have you found the books?

As you can see from these examples, **yes-no** questions and questions that begin with an interrogative word can be, for the most part, identical. Likewise, the choice of **do/did** in a question is the same in either type of question. This is possible because the interrogatives illustrated in the four examples are substitutes for adverbs, and since adverbs only modify, changes are not always needed in a question.

This is not the case, however, with **who** and **what**. These two interrogatives are actually pronouns that stand in place of a subject or an object in a sentence. In the following examples, an arrow (→) points out how a declarative sentence is changed to an interrogative sentence with **who** or **what**. For example:

Subject	The man is sick.	→	**Who** is sick?
Subject	A box is needed.	→	**What** is needed?
Object	They met the woman.	→	**Whom** did they meet?
Object	She broke the lamp.	→	**What** did she break?
Object	I spoke with him.	→	**With** whom did I speak?
Object	The boy sat on it.	→	**On** what did the boy sit?

In less formal style, **who** is often substituted for **whom**. This occurs even in writing, although in formal writing the appropriate use of **whom** should be applied.

Also, the placing of a preposition in front of **whom** or **what** is formal in style. In a less formal version, prepositions are placed at the end of the question and would look like this:

Who did you speak with?
What did the boy sit on?

If a possessive of **who** or **what** is required, use **whose** or **of what**.

I spoke with Tom's father.   With **whose** father did you speak?
The color of the book is red.   **Whose** color is red? (The color of **what** is red?)

Exercise

2·5

Use the underlined cue provided to determine which interrogative word applies; then write the appropriate question for the sentence.

EXAMPLE: John is a fantastic soccer player.

Who is a fantastic soccer player?

1. The attendant closed and locked <u>the gates</u> at seven sharp.

_____

2. They leave for Puerto Rico <u>at the beginning of every February</u>.

_____

3. <u>Life</u> isn't always easy to understand.

_____

4. <u>Ms. Perez's</u> two puppies got their shots today.

_____

5. They probably caught the flu <u>from the boy who coughed through the lecture</u>.

_____

6. We plan on getting to the match <u>on the subway</u>.

_____

7. That big bully threw the ball <u>on the other side of the fence</u>.

   _____

8. The girls should come home <u>right after the end of the movie</u>.

   _____

9. Andrea will dance with <u>the blond boy</u>.

   _____

10. They know about the change in plans, <u>because they received a fax from him today</u>.

   _____

Exercise
2·6

Write original sentences with the interrogatives provided.

1. why _____

2. how _____

3. whom _____

4. which _____

5. when _____

The interrogative **how** is often combined with other words to form new interrogatives. Just some of these are **how much**, **how many**, **how often**, **how old**, **how long**, and **how tall**. In sentences, they are used like this:

> **How much** does that magazine cost?
> **How often** do the girls work out?
> **How long** did you have to wait to see the doctor?
> **How tall** is the center on the basketball team?

Exercise
2·7

*Form original questions with **how** by combining it with the cues provided. Then give an appropriate answer to the question.*

EXAMPLE: many <u>How many players are there on a football team?</u>
             <u>There are eleven players on a football team.</u>

1. little

   a. _____

   b. _____

2. large

   a. _____

   b. _____

3. frequently

   a. _____

   b. _____

4. difficult

   a. _____

   b. _____

5. hot

   a. _____

   b. _____

6. strong

   a. _____

   b. _____

7. often

   a. _____

   b. _____

8. carefully

   a. _____

   b. _____

9. most

   a. _____

   b. _____

10. lazily

   a. _____

   b. _____

Questions and answers

In the previous chapter, you dealt with the types of questions that exist and how they are formed in the various tenses and with various auxiliaries. In this chapter, you will analyze the various elements of sentences to determine what kind of question is required by those elements.

Questions about all the information in a sentence

For starters, if you ask a question about an entire sentence and are not seeking specific information about a part of that sentence, you will ask a **yes-no** question.

> entire sentence → **yes-no** question

Let us assume that you wish to ask about all the information in the following sentence:

> John is the brother-in-law of the new mayor.

The question for this complete sentence is a **yes-no** question:

> Is John the brother-in-law of the new mayor?

The possible answers are as follows:

> Yes, John is the brother-in-law of the new mayor.
> No, John isn't the brother-in-law of the new mayor.

Let's look at a couple more examples of questions that inquire into all the information in a sentence:

> The new cruise ship will be one of the largest in the world.
> → Will the new cruise ship be one of the largest in the world?
> → Yes, the new cruise ship will be one of the largest in the world.
> or No, the new cruise ship won't be one of the largest in the world.

> My daughter had a baby last month.
> → Did your daughter have a baby last month?
> → Yes, my daughter had a baby last month.
> or No, my daughter didn't have a baby last month.

Write a **yes-no** *question for each of the following statements. Retain the tense of the original statement. Then answer each question once with* **yes** *and once with* **no**. *Following the* **no** *response, provide an original positive response.*

EXAMPLE: She spoke with him yesterday.

<u>Did she speak with him yesterday?</u>

<u>Yes, she spoke with him yesterday.</u>

<u>No, she didn't speak with him yesterday. She spoke with him today.</u>

1. The conductor of the orchestra studied music in New York.

   a. _____

   b. _____

   c. _____

2. The discovery of the New World changed the world forever.

   a. _____

   b. _____

   c. _____

3. There are numerous species of birds of prey in this region.

   a. _____

   b. _____

   c. _____

4. The hatchlings suffered during the cold weather.

   a. _____

   b. _____

   c. _____

5. My cousin in Cleveland won the lottery.

   a. _____

   b. _____

   c. _____

6. The performance is supposed to start at eight P.M.

   a. _____

   b. _____

   c. _____

7. The operation was a total success.

    a. _____

    b. _____

    c. _____

8. Mr. Keller's niece has great artistic ability.

    a. _____

    b. _____

    c. _____

9. Outdoor concerts are given on Mondays and Fridays.

    a. _____

    b. _____

    c. _____

10. The toddler fell asleep on the floor.

    a. _____

    b. _____

    c. _____

Questions about specific parts of a sentence

When you seek information about only a portion of a sentence, you should not use a **yes-no** question. Instead, an interrogative word is used that identifies the part of the sentence about which you are inquiring.

> question about a specific part of a sentence → interrogative word

Take note that nearly every element in a sentence can be the object of a question posed by an interrogative word. Let's look at how many questions can be derived from the following single sentence:

> Andrew Jackson came to fame after his victory at the battle of New Orleans.

Here are some possible questions:

> Who came to fame after his victory at the battle of New Orleans?
> What happened to Andrew Jackson after his victory at the battle of New Orleans?
> When did Andrew Jackson come to fame?
> Why did Andrew Jackson come to fame?
> In what city did Andrew Jackson come to fame after his victory there?
> At what battle did Andrew Jackson come to fame?
> After what event did Andrew Jackson come to fame?

And of course, a **yes-no** question can be asked about the information in the entire sentence:

Did Andrew Jackson come to fame after his victory at the battle of New Orleans?

Placing prepositions in an interrogative phrase

When you ask a question about the information in a prepositional phrase, the preposition must be included in the question. Its position in the question varies and is dependent on the tone of the question: is it formal or informal? In writing, the formal form tends to be preferred. Let's look at some prepositional phrases and how they are formed in questions:

Prepositional phrase	Interrogative	
It was hidden **in a box**.	In what was it hidden?	*formal*
	What was it hidden in?	*informal*
The letters were **from him**.	From whom were the letters?	*formal*
	Who were the letters from?	*informal*
They spoke **about the war**.	About what did they speak?	*formal*
	What did they speak about?	*informal*
The dog waits **for the boy**.	For whom does the dog wait?	*formal*
	Who does the dog wait for?	*informal*

When a prepositional phrase indicates a *location* or a *destination*, the interrogative **where** can usually replace a preposition and an interrogative. For example:

Prepositional phrase	Interrogative
They hid **in the barn**.	In what did they hide?
	What did they hide in?
	Where did they hide?
The cat slept **under the sofa**.	Under what did the cat sleep?
	What did the cat sleep under?
	Where did the cat sleep?
I traveled **to Venice**.	To what city did you travel?
	What city did you travel to?
	Where did you travel?

It is most common to use **where** in questions that inquire into location or destination, but a preposition and an interrogative can be used if you want to be precise or specific.

If someone is returning from a place, **where** and **from** are used to form the question.

He just got back from Iraq.	**Where** did he just get back **from**?
Mom returned from the store.	**Where** did Mom return **from**?

Write a separate question for each of the underlined elements in the following sentences.

EXAMPLE: The old house was covered in vines.

What was covered in vines?

In what was the old house covered?

1. The men from the home office arrived in time for the dedication.

    a. _____

    b. _____

    c. _____

2. The old bull became enraged and charged the unsuspecting visitors.

    a. _____

    b. _____

    c. _____

3. In the winter of 2008, several tourists lost their way in a dangerous blizzard.

    a. _____

    b. _____

    c. _____

4. The defendant was berated mercilessly by the angry judge.

    a. _____

    b. _____

    c. _____

5. The eager hunter bought some shells before heading out to the duck blind.

    a. _____

    b. _____

    c. _____

Combine each set of words into an appropriate sentence. Then ask a question about two elements in that sentence.

EXAMPLE: toys / lie / middle / floor

The child's toys were lying **in the middle of the floor**.

Whose toys were lying in the middle of the floor?

Where were the child's toys lying?

1. woman / think / about / problems / with / neighbors

    a. _____

    b. _____

    c. _____

2. I / jump / river / swim / opposite shore

    a. _____

    b. _____

    c. _____

3. no one / suspect / men / crimes / another state

    a. _____

    b. _____

    c. _____

4. children / songs / dances / delight / guests

    a. _____

    b. _____

    c. _____

5. nocturnal animal / prey / rabbit / mouse

    a. _____

    b. _____

    c. _____

Answer each of the following questions with a sentence containing an appropriate prepositional phrase or adverb.

1. On what day of the week is the new restaurant closed?

_____

2. The price of what is going to be more than a hundred dollars?

_____

3. What was the treasure buried in?

_____

4. With whom did Ms. Burns have that horrible argument?

_____

5. What time do you want to leave for the game?

_____

6. About what was the lecturer speaking?

_____

7. Where do you want to go on vacation next year?

_____

8. Who can you rely on in times like this?

_____

9. When do you plan on leaving for work?

_____

10. Whose house did the children have to live at?

_____

Using the word or phrase provided, write a declarative sentence. Then ask a question that can be answered with the cue word or phrase.

EXAMPLE: at night

The boys rarely went out at night.

When did the boys rarely go out?

1. recently

   a. _____

   b. _____

2. during summer vacation

   a. _____

   b. _____

3. to New England

   a. _____

   b. _____

4. in the Colorado Rockies

   a. _____

   b. _____

5. near Lake Michigan

   a. _____

   b. _____

6. Mr. Newman's

   a. _____

   b. _____

7. seldom

   a. _____

   b. _____

8. as tall as a tree

   a. _____

   b. _____

9. while visiting Canada

   a. _____

   b. _____

10. extremely beautiful

a. _____

b. _____

Answer the following questions in any appropriate way. Include the cue word or phrase provided in parentheses.

EXAMPLE: Who left for work at seven A.M.? (older)

My older brother left for work at seven A.M. as usual.

1. When can you have this project completed? (schedule)

_____

2. Is there really any difference between their two plans? (at the very least)

_____

3. Whose dissertation was rejected? (incompetent)

_____

4. What is the length of the course for this year's marathon? (obstacles)

_____

5. During what war did the Battle of the Bulge take place? (unexpected)

_____

6. What became of the young woman who wrote this beautiful letter? (in a terrible storm)

_____

7. Why does the boss always contradict me? (perfect)

_____

8. Where is the actress in this play from? (beautiful)

_____

9. Why don't you believe me? (lies and half-truths)

_____

10. Have you been involved with this person for a long time? (trust)

_____

Imperatives

Imperatives, or commands, are as important in good sentence writing as any other grammatical element. It is essential to differentiate among the various types of imperatives in order to use them appropriately and effectively.

You as the subject of an imperative

Most imperatives are made to the second-person singular or plural (**you**), although the pronoun is not stated.

> imperative form of a verb + predicate → command

Certain gruff or impolite-sounding imperatives cannot be used in every situation. Some of these are said in a casual manner, while others are said in anger or out of belligerence. For example:

Shut up!	Get out!
Be quiet!	Don't ever say that again!
Don't ever do that again!	Stop it!
Hurry up!	Leave me alone!
Shut your mouth!	Give me that!
Let go!	Take your time!

The exclamation point

Most imperatives of this nature are punctuated with an exclamation point, but imperatives can also be punctuated with a period. An exclamation point in writing is a signal that the imperative is stated with great emphasis. For example:

Stand up!	*emphatic, perhaps angry in tone*
Stand up.	*milder but still casual and a bit gruff in tone*

Other short imperatives can be written with an exclamation point when they are pleas or urgent requests. For example:

Have a heart!	Be patient!
Stand back!	Keep moving!
Don't joke about that!	Hold on tight!
Don't excite the dog!	Make some room for me!

Respond to each incident described with a gruff or angry imperative.

1. Someone approaches you menacingly and says, "I'm going to get you."

   _____

2. Someone has unlocked your diary and is reading through it.

   _____

3. Someone continues to refuse to leave your home.

   _____

4. Someone is acting foolishly and is teasing you.

   _____

5. Someone is packing a suitcase slowly although the hour of departure is near.

   _____

6. Someone is pestering you and making you annoyed.

   _____

Follow the same directions, but respond with a plea or an urgent request.

7. A child is leaning down to pet a vicious dog.

   _____

8. You're riding fast on a motorcycle and you tell your passenger to be careful.

   _____

9. You are thirsty and would like a soft drink.

   _____

10. You feel that someone should be kinder.

    _____

Please

Most imperatives are usually said with a certain amount of courtesy. The inclusion of **please** softens the tone of the command. Certainly, **please wait here** sounds nicer than **wait here**. Therefore, it is wise to include the word **please** in most commands. However, its position in a sentence and the addition or lack of a comma can change the general meaning of the sentence significantly.

If an imperative begins with **please**, it has the same meaning as when it ends with **please**.

please + imperative verb + predicate

Please + lend + me a dollar.

imperative verb + predicate + please

Lend + me a dollar +, please.

If **please** is written at the end of an imperative, as in the example just shown, it is preceded by a comma. Here are more examples:

Please sign here.	Sign here, please.
Please fill out this form.	Fill out this form, please.
Please fasten your seat belts.	Fasten your seat belts, please.

A comma placed after an initial **please** changes the courteous meaning to one that suggests impatience or exasperation. In speech, the word **please** would be followed by a pause before the imperative is given. In writing, the pause is indicated by a comma.

Courteous	Impatient
Please keep back from the fire.	Please, keep back from the fire.
Please don't feed the animals.	Please, don't feed the animals.
Please move along quickly.	Please, move along quickly.

If the imperative is meant to show impatience or exasperation, it can be punctuated with an exclamation point:

Please, control your temper!

Exercise
4·2

Using the cue word provided, write an imperative sentence twice, beginning it once with ***please*** *and ending it once with* ***please***.

EXAMPLE: stay

Please stay in your room.

Stay in your room, please.

1. enjoy

   a. _____

   b. _____

2. find

   a. _____

   b. _____

3. remember

   a. _____

   b. _____

4. choose

   a. _____

   b. _____

5. explain

   a. _____

   b. _____

6. remain

   a. _____

   b. _____

7. pretend

   a. _____

   b. _____

8. join

   a. _____

   b. _____

9. follow

   a. _____

   b. _____

10. hurry

   a. _____

   b. _____

Let's and let

While most imperatives are said to the second-person-singular or second-person-plural pronoun **you**, some can include the person giving the command. Imperatives of this type begin with the contraction **let's** (**let us**) and are followed by an infinitive phrase. Infinitive phrases that follow **let's** omit the particle word **to**. **Let's** conveys that the person giving the command will participate in the action of the command; for example, **Let's listen to some music.** In this sentence, the speaker suggests that you listen to some music, and the speaker will join you in that activity. **Let's** is the contraction of **let us**, but the uncontracted form is used less often.

> **let's + infinitive phrase**
>
> Let's + go home.

Here are a few more examples:

> **Let's take** a look at that scratch on your arm.
> **Let's work** on a new way of blocking unwanted e-mails.
> **Let's see** what's on today's agenda.

If the verb **let** is used without the contraction of **us** (**let's**), it still is an imperative, but it has a different meaning. In this case, the person giving the command is suggesting that "you" allow someone or something to perform an action. The structure consists of **let** followed by a direct object and an infinitive phrase with the particle word **to** omitted.

> **let + direct object + infinitive phrase**
>
> Let + them + sleep until ten.

For example:

Let John help you with the project.
Let me know whether you need more time for the job.
Let the problem just go away.
Let the soldiers find some shade and get a little rest.

*Rewrite the following sentences as an imperative with **let's**. Then, after adding an appropriate direct object, rewrite the imperative with **let**.*

EXAMPLE: You drove Maria to the bus station.

Let's drive Maria to the bus station.

Let Henry drive Maria to the bus station.

1. You spent about two hundred dollars.

a. _____

b. _____

2. You send Jim a text.

a. _____

b. _____

3. You should send them another e-mail.

a. _____

b. _____

4. You report the burglary to the police.

a. _____

b. _____

5. You have repaired the rickety steps.

a. _____

b. _____

6. You tried to signal the boat struggling in the swift current.

a. _____

b. _____

7. You will send for the paramedics.

a. _____

b. _____

8. You drove to the edge of the cliff.

a. _____

b. _____

9. You have to put up a privacy fence.

a. _____

b. _____

10. You solve the difficult equation.

a. _____

b. _____

How about

Another version of an imperative appears in the form of a question. It begins with the phrase **how about** and is followed by a gerund and its complement. This kind of imperative sounds more like a suggestion than a command, and since it is in the form of a question, it gives the impression that it is no command at all. Also, it includes the command giver in the action. Let's peruse some examples:

> **How about** going to the movies tonight?
> **How about** having dinner at the Bella Luna Café?
> **How about** giving me a hand with this heavy chest?

Why don't you

Yet another version of an imperative also appears in the form of a question. It begins with **why don't you** and is followed by an infinitive phrase. Unlike imperatives with **how about**, this imperative does not include the command giver in the action of the verb.

> **Why don't you** go out and play for a while?
> **Why don't you** get dressed and come down for breakfast?
> **Why don't you** think about what you just said?

If you change the pronoun **you** to **we** in this imperative, the command giver is now included in the action of the verb. For example:

> **Why don't we** try to get along a little better?
> **Why don't we** set a trap for that pesky raccoon?
> **Why don't we** take a little trip downtown and do some shopping?

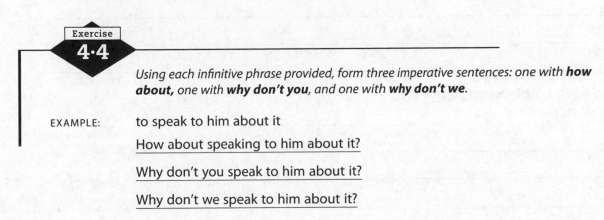

Exercise
4·4

*Using each infinitive phrase provided, form three imperative sentences: one with **how about**, one with **why don't you**, and one with **why don't we**.*

EXAMPLE: to speak to him about it

How about speaking to him about it?

Why don't you speak to him about it?

Why don't we speak to him about it?

1. to sit down under a shady tree

   a. _____

   b. _____

   c. _____

2. to come to an understanding about this matter

   a. _____

   b. _____

   c. _____

3. to let them work it out for themselves

   a. _____

   b. _____

   c. _____

4. to grant her permission to take the trip

   a. _____

   b. _____

   c. _____

5. to sing a song for Grandma

   a. _____

   b. _____

   c. _____

6. to refrain from using such language

   a. _____

   b. _____

   c. _____

7. to fertilize the fields with dung

   a. _____

   b. _____

   c. _____

8. to open a business on State Street

   a. _____

   b. _____

   c. _____

9. to register to vote in the next election

   a. _____

   b. _____

   c. _____

10. to try to behave a little better

   a. _____

   b. _____

   c. _____

Exercise 4·5

Using the cues provided, write original imperative sentences.

1. please

_____

2. let's

_____

3. let

_____

4. Please, . . . !

_____

5. how about

_____

6. why don't you

_____

7. spend more time

_____

8. work out

_____

9. Please keep . . .

_____

10. why don't

_____

Coordinating and correlative conjunctions

Conjunctions are used to combine words, phrases, or clauses. The two major types of conjunctions are coordinating conjunctions and correlative conjunctions.

word + conjunction + word
phrase + conjunction + phrase
clause + conjunction + clause

Coordinating conjunctions

Coordinating conjunctions are some of the most commonly used conjunctions. They include **and**, **but**, **or**, **nor**, **for**, **so**, and **yet**. The conjunctions **and** and **or** can be used to connect words, phrases, and clauses. For example:

John **and** Mary became engaged last night.
Working in a factory **and** working in a mine are both hard work.
Uncle Jake is snoozing on the couch, **and** Aunt Sue is working in the kitchen.

Do you want a hot dog **or** a hamburger?
Did they go fishing **or** hiking out in the forest?
We could take a trip to Canada, **or** we could save more money and go to Europe.

The other coordinating conjunctions are used primarily to combine clauses, and those clauses are separated by a comma. Let's look at some examples:

You say you love me, **but** you never hold me anymore.
She doesn't believe in me, **nor** does she understand my goals for myself.
Yes, I committed the crime, **for** there was no other way out for me.
We're out of money, **so** we've come to you for a loan.
I want you to go on this trip, **yet** I worry that you're really not old enough.

In some cases, it is possible to make the second clause "elliptical"—that is, omit a portion of the clause that is understood. This can occur if the subjects of the two clauses are identical. For example:

We could take a trip to Canada **or** save more money and go to Europe.
You say you love me **but** never hold me anymore.
She doesn't believe in me **nor** understand my goals for myself.
I want you to go on the trip **yet** worry that you're really not old enough.

When the second clause is elliptical, the comma separating the two clauses is usually omitted. In certain cases, a comma can be used to avoid confusion.

With the conjunction provided in parentheses, use the set of cue words to form two clauses of a sentence. Use the same subject in the two clauses. Then rewrite the sentence with the second clause in its elliptical form.

EXAMPLE: (and) look for / treasure / hidden / cabin / hope / become / rich

We were looking for a treasure hidden in the old cabin, and we were hoping to become rich from the discovery.

We were looking for a treasure hidden in the old cabin and hoping to become rich from the discovery.

1. (and) during vacation / spend / seashore / snorkeling / beautiful fish

   a. _____

   b. _____

2. (but) attend / reception / candidate / become ill / stay home

   a. _____

   b. _____

3. (or) stay / city / travel / Mexico / visit / relatives

   a. _____

   b. _____

4. (nor) care for / ideas / about / trust / judgment / about

   a. _____

   b. _____

5. (and) tell lies / about / ruin / friendship / with

   a. _____

   b. _____

6. (yet) give / opportunity / work / concern / lack skill / maturity

   a. _____

   b. _____

7. (but) look / beautiful / dress / satisfied / hair

   a. _____

   b. _____

Exercise 5·2

Write an appropriate completion for each of the following sentences.

1. The lawyers met for hours behind closed doors, but

_____

2. Can you spend the weekend with us in Miami, or

_____

3. The soldiers were sweating from the intense heat, for

_____

4. You've really bungled this project, so

_____

5. The dean has authorized a scholarship for her, yet

_____

6. _____, but we continued on our journey as though nothing were wrong.

7. _____, or we might have to sell our house.

8. _____, for an honest man doesn't have to explain himself.

9. _____, so the investors decided to rely on his judgment.

10. _____, yet there still is room for doubt.

Exercise 5·3

Write original sentences with the conjunctions provided.

1. or _____

2. nor _____

3. for _____

4. so _____

5. yet _____

Correlative conjunctions

Correlative conjunctions are pairs of words that function together to combine other words or phrases in a sentence. The words in the pairs of conjunctions cannot be separated and used alone; to have the intended meaning, they must be used together. The following pairs are used as correlative conjunctions: **as/as**, **both/and**, **either/or**, **hardly/when**, **if/then**, **neither/nor**, **no sooner/than**, **not only/but also**, **rather/than**, **scarcely/when**, and **whether/or**.

Standard forms

The correlative conjunctions can combine two subjects to form a compound subject. They can link two direct objects or two verb phrases. They can even combine two complete clauses. The following sentences illustrate combined subjects:

> **Both** Frank **and** his brother worked in their father's shop.
> **Either** the weather **or** the bad road caused the accident.

These example sentences illustrate combined clauses:

> I had **hardly** begun to speak **when** the power went out.
> **If** you are going to argue with me, (**then**) I'm going to leave.
> He is **as** good an athlete **as** he is a (good) student.

In the following sentence, **neither/nor** combines two objects:

> You have **neither** a driver's license **nor** the skill to drive a car.

The following example illustrates combined verb phrases:

> We would **rather** play soccer **than** go for a run.

The conjunction pair **whether/or** combines two phrases or clauses.

> Has she decided **whether** to take one suitcase **or** two?
> His interest in music was dependent upon **whether** he was listening to a favorite song **or** was being forced to practice the violin.

It is common to omit **then** from the correlative pair **if/then**, because its meaning is understood.

> **If** it rains, **then** we'll stay home.   *or* **If** it rains, we'll stay home.

When using **whether/or**, you can combine two clauses or phrases. The clause following **or** can be elliptical because its meaning is understood.

> I don't know **whether** to go on a diet **or** not (to go on a diet).

Exercise
5·4

Complete each sentence that follows with any appropriate phrase.

1. The little girl is as sweet as _____.

2. Both Laura and Jane _____.

3. No sooner had she left my apartment _____.

4. You should either get up early or _____.

5. If what you say is true, _____.

6. No sooner had Tom said, "I love you," than _____.

7. Have you decided whether to _____?

8. Scarcely had I opened my eyes, when _____.

9. No sooner _____ than Joe showed up.

10. _____ nor any interest in this project.

Singular or plural verb

When certain correlative conjunctions combine two subjects, it is the subject closer to the verb that determines whether the verb will have a singular or a plural ending. For example:

Neither John nor his **brother** has a girlfriend right now.   *singular*
Neither John nor his **sisters** have ever gone abroad.   *plural*

It is either Bill or his **friend** who speaks German.   *singular*
It is either Bill or his **friends** who speak German.   *plural*

In the case of the correlative conjunction **both/and**, the conjunction **and** tells you that a compound subject is formed, and therefore the verb will always be a plural.

Both Mary and her sister are taking ballet.
Both Mary and her three sisters are taking ballet.

Exercise
5·5

Write original sentences with the correlative conjunctions provided. Include the cue word in parentheses in each of your sentences.

EXAMPLE: both/and (wolf)

Both a wolf and a coyote prey on smaller animals.

1. either/or (diplomat)

_____

2. neither/nor (famous)

_____

3. if/then (war)

_____

4. not only/but also (careless)

_____

5. hardly/when (roof)

_____

6. both/and (like)

_____

7. whether/or (to study)

_____

8. scarcely/when (snake)

_____

9. rather/than (run away)

_____

10. no sooner/than (bear)

_____

Using the cues provided, write complete sentences. If part of a correlative conjunction is provided, include the missing part in your sentence.

EXAMPLE: both Both Tom and Laura speak fluent French.

1. and _____

2. but _____

3. for _____

4. so _____

5. either _____

6. not only _____

7. no sooner _____

8. rather _____

9. scarcely _____

10. if _____

Subordinating conjunctions and conjunctive adverbs

Subordinating conjunctions combine two clauses much in the same way as coordinating conjunctions, but there is a significant difference between the two types of conjunctions. A clause that follows a subordinating conjunction cannot stand alone and is dependent on a main clause to complete its meaning. These clauses are often called **dependent clauses**.

main clause + subordinating conjunction + dependent clause

Subordinating conjunctions

Some of the most commonly used subordinating conjunctions are listed here:

after	even though	that
although	how	though
as	if	till
as if	inasmuch as	unless
as long as	in order that	until
as much as	lest	when
as soon as	now that	whenever
as though	provided (that)	where
because	since	wherever
before	so that	while
even if	than	why

If a sentence begins with a clause introduced by a subordinating conjunction, that clause will be separated from the main clause by a comma. For example:

After I received the horrible news, I fell into a deep depression.
If you can lend us a hand, we can pay you a few dollars.
When the train's horn began to sound, we knew there was trouble ahead.

If the clause introduced by a subordinating conjunction follows the main clause, a comma is not required.

I don't know **why** you treat me this way.
We'll wait in the car **until** the rain stops.
The young couple hurried to the bank **as soon as** they received the check.

The conjunction **because** *tends* to use a comma to separate its clause from the main clause whether it stands at the beginning of the sentence or follows the main clause. However, when the subordinate clause follows the main clause, the use of a comma is *optional*, particularly when the verb in the main clause is negated.

> You can't go back to class yet(,) **because** you still have the flu.
> **Because** you got drunk, your license has been revoked.

Exercise
6·1

Using the conjunction provided, write an appropriate clause to complete each of the following sentences.

EXAMPLE: If <u>you help me with the dishes</u>, I will help you with your homework.

1. When _____ , she dropped the vase she was dusting.

2. Although _____ , I'm still in love with you.

3. As long as _____ , we will stand beside you.

4. In order that _____ , you will have to have a complete physical examination.

5. Wherever _____ , you will find your success in life.

6. Even though _____ , I am willing to work out our differences.

7. Unless _____ , you won't be welcome in this house again.

8. Providing that _____ , she will be allowed to enter graduate school.

9. After _____ , they can start getting ready for bed.

10. Since _____ , you have become part of our family.

The conjunction **since** has two meanings and, therefore, is used in two different ways:

◆ The reason for an action

> **Since** you refuse to explain your behavior, I have to side with Mary.
> **Since** there is little doubt about his guilt, the judge fined him a hundred dollars.

◆ A time in the past when something occurred

> **Since** you first arrived on campus, I've had my eye on you.
> **Since** their son left home, they haven't heard a word from him.

Positioning for emphasis

The clause that appears first in a sentence is usually the one that is emphasized. This is true of both subordinating clauses and main clauses.

When he finally got home, he stretched out on the sofa to rest.   *emphasis on* when he finally got home

He stretched out on the sofa to rest when he finally got home.   *emphasis on* he stretched out on the sofa to rest

Exercise
6·2

Using the conjunction provided, write an appropriate clause to complete each sentence that follows. Then rewrite the sentence by placing the subordinate clause at the beginning of the sentence.

EXAMPLE: He won't get paid unless <u>he finishes the job.</u>

<u>Unless he finishes the job, he won't get paid.</u>

1. I'm going to make some breakfast while _____ .

   _____

2. She always visits the museums whenever _____ .

   _____

3. The jurors couldn't believe the witness as long as _____ .

   _____

4. Can you set the table for me after _____ ?

   _____

5. His mother was less concerned about him now that _____ .

   _____

6. They resolved the problem before _____ .

   _____

7. John opened a savings account once _____ .

   _____

8. You will receive your inheritance assuming that _____ .

   _____

9. The young actors will be fired unless _____ .

   _____

10. You can't watch television until _____ .

   _____

Exercise

6·3

Complete each sentence that follows with any appropriate clause. Use a subordinating conjunction that makes sense in the context of the sentence.

EXAMPLE: Margaret burst into tears <u>when he asked her to marry him</u>.

1. _____ , it stopped raining and the sun came out again.

2. _____ , he worked in France as a translator.

3. _____ , I'm going to take away all your privileges.

4. _____ , the hikers decided to return home early.

5. _____ , no one will trust the woman.

6. _____ , he was one of the best-liked boys in school.

7. _____ , you'll never get into college.

8. _____ , the bank will make her a loan of a thousand dollars.

9. We'd stay in Paris longer _____ .

10. By the end of the day, they were exhausted _____ .

Exercise

6·4

Using the conjunctions provided, write original sentences that contain a clause introduced by a subordinating conjunction and a main clause. Place the subordinating clause before or after the main clause.

EXAMPLE: although

Although her health had been failing, the queen attended the ceremony.

OR

The queen attended the ceremony although her health had been failing.

1. whenever

_____

2. as long as

_____

3. as if

_____

4. assuming that

_____

5. because

_____

6. where

_____

7. in order that

_____

8. since (*a time in the past when something occurred*)

_____

9. since (*the reason for an action*)

_____

10. how

_____

Tenses

You may have noticed that a variety of tenses and various auxiliary verbs can be used in both subordinating and main clauses. Let's look at some specific examples of how tenses vary. In the present tense and in the past tense with most conjunctions, both clauses are in the same tense.

Present   When I **travel** in Europe, I **prefer** to stay in small hotels.
Past   When I **traveled** in Europe, I **preferred** to stay in small hotels.

The other tenses and the progressive tenses are not so reliable. One tense may be used in one clause and another tense in the other clause. For example, with **when** and **while**, one clause can be in the progressive tense and the other not.

I **was sleeping** in the living room when I **heard** a strange noise.
While I **was sleeping** in the living room, I **heard** a strange noise.

She **had been preparing** supper when the kitchen door **flew open**.
While she **had been preparing** supper, the kitchen door **flew open**.

Notice in the preceding examples that in the progressive tense, the past perfect can substitute for the past tense. This fact can be further illustrated by comparing the following pairs of sentences with those just illustrated:

I **had been sleeping** in the living room when I **heard** a strange noise.
While I **had been sleeping** in the living room, I **heard** a strange noise.

She **was preparing** supper when the kitchen door **flew open**.
While she **was preparing** supper, the kitchen door **flew open**.

When a main clause is in the future tense, the present tense is used in the subordinating clause.

future tense in + conjunction + present tense in
main clause   dependent clause

or

conjunction + present tense in + future tense in
dependent clause   main clause

I **will phone** you immediately when I **arrive** in town.
Once the new tenant **is** settled in, we**'ll invite** her over for coffee.
I **will support** you as long as you **need** my help.

However, if there is an auxiliary other than a future-tense auxiliary (**shall**, **will**) in the main clause, that auxiliary is used in its present- or past-tense form. Such auxiliaries are **can**, **could**, **must**, **would**, and **should**. The exceptions to this rule are the auxiliaries that are composed of a verb followed by **to**; for example: **be able to**, **have to**, **want to**, **be supposed to**, **ought to**, **need to**, **allowed to**. These auxiliaries can be in the future tense in the main clause. Compare the following pairs of sentences:

I **can phone** you when I **arrive** in town.
I **will be able to phone** you when I **arrive** in town.

Once she **is** settled in, we **must invite** her over for coffee.
Once she **is** settled in, we **will have to invite** her over for coffee.

Until he **gets** a job, Maria **should have** nothing to do with him.
Until he **gets** a job, Maria **won't be allowed to have** anything to do with him.

If the main clause is an imperative, the subordinating clause can be in the present tense or the present perfect tense, depending on the meaning required:

- Present-tense subordinating clause

  Stand up straight while I **measure** your inseam.
  Come right home after the game **is** over.
  Think of me here in Iowa when you**'re vacationing** in sunny Mexico.

- Present-tense or present-perfect-tense subordinating clause following **after**

  Sign on the dotted line after you **read** through the contract.
  Sign on the dotted line after you **have read** through the contract.

The action of the imperative in the preceding example is carried out *after* another action has been completed. Although the present tense is often used for this meaning, it is the present perfect tense that is more common to describe an action in the past that follows the preposition **after**. For example:

Set the table after you **do** your homework.
Set the table after you **have done** your homework.

Let's light a fire after we **finish** cleaning the living room.
Let's light a fire after we **have finished** cleaning the living room.

Complete each sentence that follows with an appropriate clause and in the needed tense.

EXAMPLE: She will forget about him <u>after enough time goes by.</u>

1. Open the front door _____ .

2. _____ , we can work on your résumé together.

3. While he was studying at the library, _____ .

4. _____ , take the dog out for a walk.

5. When Ms. Harris goes on vacation, _____ .

6. Whenever Robert plays his clarinet, _____ .

7. Once he finally understood what she meant, _____ .

8. Please have your passport and visa ready _____ .

9. _____ if that is truly what you want me to do.

10. Inasmuch as there is so little time left, _____ .

Using the conjunctions provided, write original sentences that contain two clauses, one of which should be in the future tense.

EXAMPLE: while <u>While you clean up the kitchen, I'll get the kids ready for bed.</u>

1. until _____

2. once _____

3. if _____

4. before _____

5. unless _____

6. while _____

7. when _____

8. after _____

9. as long as _____

10. once _____

Conjunctive adverbs

Certain adverbial expressions can function as conjunctions. They are called **conjunctive adverbs**, and they combine two clauses just as other conjunctions do. However, there is a different approach to punctuation with conjunctive adverbs: a semicolon precedes a conjunctive adverb, and a comma follows it. Here are some commonly used conjunctive adverbs:

after all	in addition	next
also	incidentally	nonetheless
as a result	indeed	on the contrary
besides	in fact	on the other hand
consequently	in other words	otherwise
finally	instead	still
for example	likewise	then
furthermore	meanwhile	therefore
hence	moreover	thus
however	nevertheless	

Use conjunctive adverbs to combine two clauses that are closely linked by meaning or intent. For example:

Robert spoke out of turn; **nonetheless,** his statement made sense, and everyone agreed with him.
My daughter is quite shy; **however,** she is an aggressive athlete when playing soccer.
You have to pay your back rent immediately; **otherwise,** I'll be forced to evict you.
Your erratic driving caused the accident; **furthermore,** I'm certain I smelled alcohol on your breath.

Exercise 6·7

Combine the following pairs of sentences with any appropriate conjunctive adverb.

EXAMPLE: Jake lied. His father was forced to punish him.

Jake lied; therefore, his father was forced to punish him.

1. Tom was lounging under a tree. The other boys were loading rocks onto the truck.

_____

2. The woman stole his watch and ring. She attempted to take a credit card from his pocket.

_____

3. The operation was a miserable failure. The poor woman died on the operating table.

_____

4. I was supposed to go to class. I decided to go to the river for a swim.

_____

5. Mr. Helms collects old coins. He has several rare gold pieces from Spain.

_____

6. There will be a test tomorrow. You'll also have a lengthy assignment for over the weekend.

      _____

7. The woman didn't understand that it was a crime. She was probably not in her right mind.

      _____

8. Jim drank too much, spent too much, and caroused too much. He acted like a jackass.

      _____

9. You place the chemicals in a beaker. You light the Bunsen burner.

      _____

10. Don't be afraid to ask him for a loan. He can afford it.

      _____

Unlike the case with other conjunctions, conjunctive adverbs work best when they follow the main clause. Also, in contrast to subordinating clauses, clauses that follow conjunctive adverbs make complete sense and can stand alone. Compare the following:

Clause following a conjunctive adverb	Subordinating clause
Finally, he spoke up about the idea.	When he spoke up about the idea
Meanwhile, Bill worked on the car.	Since Bill worked on the car
For example, Einstein was a poor student.	Although Einstein was a poor student
In fact, I was once in Brazil.	Whether I was once in Brazil

Exercise
6·8

Complete each sentence that follows with an appropriate clause.

EXAMPLE: He waited an hour for a table; however, the wait was worth it, for the food was delicious.

1. _____ ; nonetheless, I stayed through the whole concert.

2. _____ ; besides, she was a wonderful dancer.

3. The storm was battering their tent; nevertheless, _____ .

4. They were swimming for their lives; finally, _____ .

5. He was a well-known thief and liar; indeed, _____ .

6. _____ ; for example, there is evidence of climate change.

7. _____ ; furthermore, I have proof that her documents are forgeries.

8. The children can play several instruments; in fact, _____ .

9. Mr. Dean didn't participate in the discussion; instead, _____ .

10. Your grades have to improve very soon; otherwise, _____ .

Using the conjunctive adverbs provided, write original sentences that contain two clauses.

EXAMPLE: however

I can't come to your wedding; however, my son will be there to cheer you on.

1. besides

_____

2. nonetheless

_____

3. still

_____

4. consequently

_____

5. thus

_____

6. meanwhile

_____

7. otherwise

_____

8. therefore

_____

9. incidentally

_____

10. moreover

_____

11. in other words

_____

12. in fact

_____

13. as a result

_____

14. also

_____

15. on the other hand

_____

Write original sentences with the following conjunctions provided. Note that these conjunctions are of various types: coordinating, subordinating, correlative, and conjunctive adverbs.

1. although

_____

2. but

_____

3. yet

_____

4. unless

_____

5. since

_____

6. accordingly

_____

7. providing that

_____

8. in addition

_____

9. either/or

_____

10. as if

_____

Pronouns

In the category of pronouns, people tend to be most familiar with personal pronouns, since these parts of speech are widely used in the English language. Other types of pronouns also exist, however, and they must be identified and practiced in order for you to be able to use them well in sentence writing. This chapter addresses the following types of pronouns: personal pronouns, relative pronouns, demonstrative pronouns, reflexive pronouns, indefinite pronouns, reciprocal pronouns, and intensive pronouns.

All pronouns are used as a replacement for a form of a noun. For example:

- Pronoun as a subject

    the man is → **he** is

- Pronoun as an object

    we saw **the man** → we saw **him**

- Possessive pronoun

    the man's → **his**

Personal pronouns

The personal pronouns have a subjective form, an objective from, and a possessive form. The subjective form is used in place of a noun subject of a sentence. The objective form is used in place of a noun serving as either a direct object, an indirect object, or the object of a preposition. The possessive form replaces a possessive noun formed with an apostrophe plus *s* (for example, **Bill's**) or in a prepositional phrase introduced by **of** (for example, **of Bill**). The personal pronouns are as follows:

SUBJECTIVE	OBJECTIVE	POSSESSIVE
I	me	my/mine
you	you	your/yours
he	him	his/his
she	her	her/hers
it	it	its/its
we	us	our/ours
they	them	their/theirs
who	whom	whose/whose
what	what	whose/whose

When a possessive modifies a noun, the first possessive form in the preceding list of pairs is used:

> **My** car is new.
> **Her** books were on the floor.
> **Their** tent blew over in the wind.

When the possessive is used in place of the possessive word and the noun it modifies, the noun is omitted, and the second form of the pairs is used.

> **Mine** is new.
> **Hers** were on the floor.
> **Theirs** blew over in the wind.

It is only the third-person pronouns (**he**, **she**, **it**, **they**, **who**, and **what**) that are substitutions for a noun. **He**, **she**, and **it** replace singular nouns.

> **The doctor** is young.   **He** is young.
> **Their daughter** was ill.   **She** was ill.
> **Jim** opened the cage.   **He** opened it.

They replaces plural nouns—both animate and inanimate.

> Are **the boys** home?   Are **they** home?
> Did you meet **our visitors**?   Did you meet **them**?

Both **who** and **what** are used in questions.

> **Jack** broke his arm.   **Who** broke his arm?
> The dog ate **the pie**.   **What** did the dog eat?

The first- and second-person pronouns (**I**, **you**, **we**) are not replacements for nouns but rather function on their own. However, **I** can be combined with nouns or other pronouns, and that combination can be replaced by a form of **we**. For example:

> **Jane and I** live on the same street.   **We** live on the same street.
> The girls saw **Tom and me**.   The girls saw **us**.
> **You and I** will always be friends.   **We** will always be friends.
> **She and I** started a club.   **We** started a club.

Exercise

7·1

A pronoun serves as the subject in each of the following sentences. Using that pronoun as your cue, write one sentence with that pronoun serving as a direct or indirect object; write a second sentence using the pronoun as the object of a preposition; and write a third sentence using the pronoun as a possessive. Link the content of each sentence so that you create a simple story line.

EXAMPLE: She developed a friendship with John.

Did John take her out on a date?

Not really, but John spoke with her every day.

Her father never really grew to like John.

1. They broke down on a regular basis.

    a. _____

    b. _____

    c. _____

2. It destroyed several houses on the edge of town.

    a. _____

    b. _____

    c. _____

3. We never allowed the dogs in the dining room during meals.

    a. _____

    b. _____

    c. _____

4. I want to travel to Mexico during winter vacation.

    a. _____

    b. _____

    c. _____

5. You bought new clothes and shoes but never went to the party.

    a. _____

    b. _____

    c. _____

6. He had to laugh when he saw his brother dressed as a clown.

    a. _____

    b. _____

    c. _____

7. She caught a bad cold and had to stay home a few days.

    a. _____

    b. _____

    c. _____

Relative pronouns

Relative pronouns are used to combine two sentences that contain identical nouns or pronouns. The sentence in which the noun is replaced by a relative pronoun becomes a subordinating clause. As such, that clause cannot stand alone; it functions as part of the main clause. The person and number of the antecedent of the relative pronoun will determine the person and number of the relative pronoun.

    person and number of antecedent → person and number of relative pronoun

The English relative pronouns are **who**, **whom**, **whose**, **which**, **that**, and an elliptical form, in which the relative pronoun is omitted but understood. The forms of **who** and **which** are used to introduce a *nonrestrictive* relative clause—that is, a clause that gives *parenthetical information*. Nonrestrictive relative clauses are set off from the rest of the sentence by commas. **That** introduces a *restrictive* relative clause—that is, a clause that defines the antecedent in the main clause. Let's look at some example sentences:

- Nonrestrictive relative clauses

  He met the mayor, **who** was elected in a landslide.

The primary information is that *he met the mayor*. The writer of this sentence is giving incidental information (*the mayor was elected in a landslide*) that is not necessarily pertinent to the fact that *he met the mayor*.

  She approached the officer, **whom** her brother knew from college.

The primary information is that *she approached the officer*. The writer of this sentence is giving incidental information (*her brother knew the officer from college*) that is not necessarily pertinent to the fact that *she approached the officer*.

  I opened the ledger, **which** had two large ink stains on it.

The primary information is that *I opened the ledger*. The writer of this sentence is giving incidental information (*the ledger had two large ink stains on it*) that is not necessarily pertinent to the fact that *I opened the ledger*.

The relative clauses just illustrated merely provide parenthetical information; the information is not necessary for the meaning of the main clause. Those clauses could be omitted, because they do not enhance the meaning of the main clause:

  He met the mayor.
  She approached the officer.
  I opened the ledger.

- Restrictive relative clauses

  He met the mayor **that** was accused of unethical practices.

He didn't meet just any mayor. The relative clause explains more about its antecedent: *this mayor was accused of unethical practices*.

  She approached the officer **that** had given her a ticket.

She didn't approach just any officer. The relative clause explains more about its antecedent: *this officer had given her a ticket*.

  I opened the ledger **that** was hidden in the back of my boss's closet.

I didn't open just any ledger. The relative clause explains more about its antecedent: *this ledger was hidden in the back of my boss's closet*.

When writing sentences with relative clauses in them, it is necessary to choose the appropriate relative pronoun. If you wish to make a parenthetical statement, choose a nonrestrictive relative pronoun. If you wish to add information that explains the antecedent in the main clause, choose a restrictive relative pronoun. For example:

David danced with the woman, **who** has a summer house on the shore.
David danced with the woman **that** had been flirting with him.
David danced with the woman **who** had been flirting with him.

Be aware that **who** can function as a restrictive relative pronoun and can replace **that**.

◆ Elliptical relative pronouns

I found the little ashtray (**that**) you made in junior high school.
We finally arrived at the corner (**that**) John had been waiting on for hours.
Here's the jacket (**that**) I bought yesterday.

Notice that the word **that** can be omitted in these clauses only when they are used as objects. When **that** is used as the subject of the clause, it must be retained.

Here's the jacket **that** was made in France.   *subject*
Have you met our new neighbors **that** live on Hyde Street?   *subject*

An elliptical relative pronoun can be derived from a clause containing either **that** or **which**. However, when the relative pronoun is omitted, the tone of the clause becomes restrictive.

Here's the jacket, **which** I bought yesterday.   → Here's the jacket I bought yesterday.
Here's the jacket **that** I bought yesterday.   → Here's the jacket I bought yesterday.

It is correct to use **whose** to refer to either an animate or an inanimate antecedent. With inanimate antecedents, the prepositional phrase **of which** can replace **whose**. For example:

◆ Animate antecedents

Tim liked the girl, **whose** eyes were following him wherever he went.
Have you interviewed the man **whose** house burned down?

◆ Inanimate antecedents

She bought a sweater, **whose** dark color didn't flatter her.
She bought a sweater, the dark color **of which** didn't flatter her.

The judge studied the document, **whose** content was extremely vague.
The judge studied the document, the content **of which** was extremely vague.

Prepositions in relative clauses require a special look. Their position is not static; they can occupy two different places in the clause. In formal style, the preposition precedes a nonrestrictive relative pronoun. For example:

The lawyer, **from whom** he received the information, is under investigation.
I cannot explain the circumstances, **under which** she gradually lost her wealth.
They innocently hiked toward the woods, **in which** cannibals were said to dwell.

In a less formal style, the preposition can be placed at the end of the clause:

The lawyer, **whom** he received the information **from**, is under investigation.

In a still less formal style, the correct use of **whom** is avoided:

The lawyer, **who** he received the information **from**, is under investigation.

When **that** and **who(m)** are used as restrictive relative pronouns, prepositions always appear at the end of the relative clause. This is also true with elliptical relative pronouns.

The dress **that** she slipped into was much too big for her.
The dress she slipped into was much too big for her.

That's the old man **whom** Thomas works for.
That's the old man Thomas works for.

Exercise 7·2

Complete each sentence that follows with an appropriate nonrestrictive relative clause.

EXAMPLE: Henry ordered a cheese pizza, <u>which is not his girlfriend's favorite food</u>.

1. The soldiers stormed the fort, _____ .

2. We spent a week in the capital, _____ .

3. I'd like to introduce you to our new coach, _____ .

4. Dr. Flores, _____ , has to return to Madrid.

5. Can you explain this formula, _____ ?

Follow the same directions, but provide a restrictive relative clause.

6. He hurried up to the boys _____ .

7. I need a laptop _____ .

8. The man _____ is a friend of mine.

9. I'd prefer to speak to the clerk _____ .

10. Send me a copy of the message _____ .

Exercise 7·3

Complete each sentence that follows with (a) a clause that is introduced by a preposition, (b) a nonrestrictive clause that places the preposition at the end of the clause, (c) a restrictive clause with a preposition, and (d) an elliptical pronoun with a preposition.

EXAMPLE: He found a large chest

a. <u>, in which someone had hidden a map.</u>

b. <u>, which he found some money in.</u>

c. <u>that a cat was sleeping on.</u>

d. <u>his father had paid a hundred dollars for.</u>

1. The girls had to find accommodations in a village

a. _____

b. _____

c. _____

d. _____

2. Mr. Dean hoped to speak with the owners

   a. _____

   b. _____

   c. _____

   d. _____

3. She made her way to the bed

   a. _____

   b. _____

   c. _____

   d. _____

4. Sally believed she was in love with the actor

   a. _____

   b. _____

   c. _____

   d. _____

5. I avoid meetings

   a. _____

   b. _____

   c. _____

   d. _____

Demonstrative pronouns

The singular demonstrative pronouns are **this** and **that**. **This** refers to someone or something nearby or part of the present topic of conversation. **That** points to someone or something in the distance or referred to in the past. Their plural forms are **these** and **those** and refer, respectively, to something nearby or in the distance. These pronouns also function as adjectives.

> **located nearby + *this/these***
>
> **located in the distance + *that/those***

This fellow is in a lot of trouble.	*He is nearby. We're talking about him now.*
That fellow was rather arrogant.	*He is in the distance. We talked about him earlier.*
These people are friends of mine.	*They are nearby. We're talking about them now.*
Those people work for Mr. Paine.	*They are in the distance. We talked about them earlier.*

When these pronouns are not accompanied by a noun, they function as pronouns rather than as adjectives, but their meaning of closeness or distance from a person or thing is maintained.

This is the one I want.
That was the last one.

I borrowed **these** from Jim.
Were **those** once a different color?

As is true of other pronouns, demonstrative pronouns can be subjects or objects. To indicate a possessive, a demonstrative pronoun becomes the object of the preposition **of**. Here are examples:

This really wasn't necessary.	*subject*
Did you buy **those** in Mexico?	*object*
We spoke about **that** a moment ago.	*object of preposition*
What is the meaning of **this**?	*possession with **of***

Exercise
7·4

Write two original sentences: one using the cue word provided as a modifier of a noun, and one using the cue word as a pronoun.

EXAMPLE: this

This puppy is the last of the litter.

This makes me very mad!

1. this

    a. _____

    b. _____

2. that

    a. _____

    b. _____

3. these

    a. _____

    b. _____

4. those

    a. _____

    b. _____

Reflexive pronouns

Reflexive pronouns are used only as objects and never as subjects of a sentence. They can be direct objects, indirect objects, or the objects of prepositions.

He cut **himself** shaving.	*direct object*
He bought **himself** some new ties.	*indirect object*
He was talking to **himself**.	*object of preposition*

Compare the English personal pronouns with their reflexive-pronoun counterparts:

PERSONAL PRONOUNS	REFLEXIVE PRONOUNS
I	myself
you	yourself
he	himself
she	herself
it	itself
we	ourselves
you	yourselves
they	themselves

When the subject and object are different persons or things, the object is a personal pronoun. For example:

The **man** asked **her** what happened.
We bought **them** some ice cream.

It is when the subject and object are the same person or thing that a reflexive pronoun is used.

The **man** asked **himself** what happened.
We bought **ourselves** some ice cream.

Exercise

7·5

Write two sentences with the reflexive pronoun indicated and the cue words provided in parentheses. In your first sentence, use the reflexive as a direct object. In your second sentence, use the reflexive as an indirect object.

EXAMPLE: himself (illness / watch)

Despite a long illness, the elderly man carried himself well.

Tom wants to buy himself a new watch.

1. herself (spring / ring)

    a. _____

    b. _____

2. yourself (rarely / soon)

    a. _____

    b. _____

3. ourselves (dinner / dessert)

    a. _____

    b. _____

4. myself (angrily / similar)

    a. _____

    b. _____

5. themselves (sandwiches / wine)

a. _____

b. _____

Using the first cue provided, write a sentence with that cue as the object of a preposition. Then, using the reflexive pronoun provided, write a sentence with that pronoun as the object of a preposition.

EXAMPLE: sister / herself

Maria is going to buy a used car for her sister.

Maria is going to buy a used car for herself.

6. grandfather / himself

a. _____

b. _____

7. soldier / yourselves

a. _____

b. _____

8. flight attendant / myself

a. _____

b. _____

9. dancer / herself

a. _____

b. _____

10. guests / themselves

a. _____

b. _____

Indefinite pronouns

The indefinite pronouns have a unique function. They act in a sentence like other pronouns—that is, they are substitutions for nouns; however, the indefinite pronouns are not a replacement for a *specific noun*. Instead, they refer to *anyone*, *everyone*, or *no one in particular*. Here are some of the most commonly used indefinite pronouns that are always singular:

anyone/anybody   neither
each   no one/nobody
either   one
everyone/everybody   someone/somebody
much

Each pronoun in the four pairs of indefinite pronouns (**anyone/anybody, everyone/everybody, no one/nobody, someone/somebody**) is identical in meaning to its companion pronoun.

Anyone can play this game.   → **Anybody** can play this game.
No one understands me.   → **Nobody** understands me.

Also, do not confuse the indefinite pronoun **one** (a number) with the personal pronoun **one** (*a person*).

Indefinite   **One** of you will have to stay on duty tonight.
Personal   **One** might at first assume that his theory
                          is correct.

It's important to recognize these pronouns as singular, because some of them are used with prepositional phrases that can contain a plural. This construction sometimes causes confusion and results in the use of a plural verb where a singular verb is needed.

Each of the dismissed employees **receives** a termination bonus.

Since **each** is a singular, the singular verb **receives** is needed in this sentence. The plural noun in the prepositional phrase **of the dismissed employees** is not the subject of the sentence.

Here is another example:

One of you **has** to take responsibility.

Since **one** is a singular, the singular verb **has** is needed in this sentence. The plural pronoun **you** is not the subject of the sentence.

Even when more than one person or thing is understood, these pronouns still always use only a singular verb. For example:

These two ties are the right price, but **neither** really **appeals** to me.

A few indefinite pronouns are plural, such as **both, few, many**, and **several**, and they require a plural verb when used as the subject of a sentence. For example:

Both of these women **are** candidates for mayor.
Few understand his motives.
Many of his opponents **lie** about his record.

There are also indefinite pronouns that are considered either singular or plural:

all   most
any   none
more   some

The choice of a singular or plural verb with these indefinite pronouns depends on their usage in the sentence and on any accompanying prepositional phrase:

◆ Singular

All is lost!
You can take the last piece of pie. **More is** coming.
Don't eat the whole cake. **Some is** for Bill.

◆ Plural

I met John's fraternity brothers. **Most are** quite nice.
All of the children **have had** their inoculations.
There are several magazines on the floor, but **none are** mine.

EXERCISE
7·6

Using the indefinite pronoun provided, write an original sentence with the pronoun as the subject of the sentence.

1. much _____

2. either _____

3. each _____

4. neither _____

5. one _____

6. everybody _____

7. no one _____

8. few of them _____

9. many _____

10. each of the contestants _____

Reciprocal pronouns

There are only two reciprocal pronouns: **one another** and **each other**. Either one is correct, and each can replace the other in a sentence. They are used to combine two sentences that say that two persons or things are carrying out the same action. For example:

John loves Mary. Mary loves John.   → John and Mary love **one another**.
The dog glares at the cat. The cat glares   → The dog and cat glare at **each other**.
    at the dog.
She kissed me. I kissed her.   → We kissed **each other**.

When pronouns are used in pairs of sentences as in the last example (**She kissed me. I kissed her.**), the pronoun **I** indicates that a second-person-plural pronoun (**we**) will be used with a reciprocal pronoun. If the pronoun is in the third person, a third-person-plural pronoun (**they**) will be used with a reciprocal pronoun.

He sees her. She sees him.   → They see **one another**.

Intensive pronouns

Intensive pronouns are often mistaken as reflexive pronouns because they look like reflexive pronouns.

PERSONAL PRONOUNS	INTENSIVE PRONOUNS
I	myself
you	yourself
he	himself
she	herself
it	itself

we	ourselves
you	yourselves
they	themselves

Intensive pronouns function differently from reflexive pronouns. Their purpose is to emphasize the subject of the sentence. Compare the following pairs of sentences, in which the subject is emphasized in the second pair.

I believe that war with them can be avoided.
I **myself** believe that war with them can be avoided.

You said that you could afford it.
You **yourself** said that you could afford it.

They are the ones to blame.
They **themselves** are the ones to blame.

Exercise
7·7

Rewrite each sentence that follows with the appropriate intensive pronoun.

1. William tried to free the car from the muddy rut.

_____

2. Several of the men heard the strange sounds in the attic.

_____

3. I longed to return to my homeland.

_____

4. Ms. Thomas and I were rather good dancers.

_____

5. The administration is responsible for our improved economy.

_____

6. Nancy broke down in tears upon hearing the news.

_____

7. You tried to get some help for them.

_____

8. He felt ashamed for what had happened that day.

_____

9. They attempted to exploit the situation.

_____

Prepositions

Prepositions are used to introduce a prepositional phrase that ends with a noun phrase or pronoun.

preposition + object of preposition

from + the old man

Some prepositions can also function as adverbs or conjunctions. Following is a list of the most commonly used English prepositions:

about	below	from	through
above	beneath	in	throughout
across	beside	into	till
after	besides	like	to
against	between	near	toward
along	beyond	of	under
among	by	off	until
around	despite	on	up
at	down	out	with
before	during	over	within
behind	for	since	without

There is a significant difference between **beside** and **besides**. Use **beside** when you mean *near* or *next to*. Use **besides** when you mean *in addition to* or *other than*. For example:

He stood **beside** her bed.   *He stood next to her bed.*
No one cared **besides** Jack.   *No one cared other than Jack.*

The prepositions **till** and **until** can be used interchangeably.

You have to wait **till** noon.   = You have to wait **until** noon.
They worked **till** the next morning.   = They worked **until** the next morning.

Compound prepositions

Some prepositions are called *compound prepositions* because they are composed of more than one word. For example:

ahead of	in place of
because of	in regard to
by means of	in spite of
contrary to	instead of
in addition to	in view of
in back of	next to
in case of	on account of
in front of	out of
in lieu of	prior to
in light of	

Whether a preposition is a single word or a compound preposition, it is still used in the same way: to introduce a prepositional phrase.

We went straight home **after** the concert.
He arrived late **because of** the concert.

She received a gift **from** her brother.
Jane invited Alex **instead of** her brother.

A woodpecker flew **through** the window.
A stranger was standing **next to** the window.

Using *of*

The usage of the preposition **of** may seem obvious, but it requires a special explanation. The preposition **of** not only is used in several compound prepositions but also plays a role when it stands alone. The preposition **of** can serve in place of an apostrophe plus *s* to indicate a possessive. Let's look at some examples:

Preposition *of*	**Possessive**
the roar **of** the lion	the lion's roar
the father **of** the bride	the bride's father
the fur **of** the dog	the dog's fur

Although the preceding examples show the two forms used to express ownership, the apostrophe-plus-*s* form tends to be used most frequently with persons or other animate nouns, while the preposition **of** is usually preferred for inanimate objects. For example:

the quality **of** his voice	the length **of** the sidewalk
a ring **of** truth	a large stack **of** books
an explanation **of** grammar	the depth **of** the river

In some cases, the possessive form is suitable for inanimate objects (**the sidewalk's length, the river's depth**), but, in general, the preposition **of** is used to show possession with an inanimate object.

It is often the case that **of** is used as a synonym for **about**. For example:

Did you know **of** the accident?	Did you know **about** the accident?
Please don't speak **of** this again.	Please don't speak **about** this again.
Does he have knowledge **of** this case?	Does he have knowledge **about** this case?

Using the prepositional phrases provided, write original sentences.

EXAMPLE: of the story <u>The ending of the story was sad.</u>

1. of her penmanship _____

2. of the month _____

3. of mathematics _____

4. of the baby _____

5. of his tuxedo _____

6. of the carpet _____

7. of the United States _____

8. of our team _____

9. of his wife _____

10. of hunger _____

Using each of the prepositions provided once, write two original sentences that also include the cue phrase provided in parentheses.

EXAMPLE: for / on account of (his sister)

<u>Jack had a good suggestion for his sister.</u>

<u>Uncle Bill remained at home on account of his sister.</u>

1. from / in addition to (Ms. Garcia)

   a. _____

   b. _____

2. on / in back of (their mobile home)

   a. _____

   b. _____

3. about / in light of (this critical situation)

   a. _____

   b. _____

4. beyond / in place of (the wooden fence)

   a. _____

   b. _____

5. in / out of (the classroom)

   a. _____

   b. _____

6. during / prior to (their weekly meeting)

   a. _____

   b. _____

7. besides / in case of (another problem)

   a. _____

   b. _____

8. with / by means of (atomic energy)

   a. _____

   b. _____

9. till / in view of (final examinations)

   a. _____

   b. _____

10. despite / contrary to (his stated goal)

   a. _____

   b. _____

Among and between

In order to write accurately, you have to distinguish between the prepositions **among** and **between**. **Among** is used with a prepositional phrase that involves more than two persons or things. **Between** is used only with a prepositional phrase that involves just two persons or things. Let's look at some example sentences:

> **Among** the women in their department was a Ph.D. candidate from Canada.
> I just can't decide **between** these two Ph.D. candidates.

> We have always counted Andrea **among** our good friends.
> Who is that standing **between** Andrea and Michael?

> The mood **among** the members of the losing team was not good.
> The difference **between** right and wrong should be obvious to you.

Complete the following sentences with any appropriate prepositional phrase.

EXAMPLE: James had a conversation with <u>the newly arrived foreign students</u>.

1. The boys spent a lot of time alone in _____.

2. Rita sat among _____ and chatted amiably.

3. I think I'd prefer a table by _____.

4. Contrary to _____, the contract is not yet signed.

5. When the storm came, they dashed into _____.

6. Have you decided between _____?

7. The entire first floor smells of _____.

8. The boys were hiding among _____.

9. I've been living in Peru for _____.

10. The handsome young fellow stood opposite _____.

To and out

Some words function both as prepositions and as other parts of speech. As a preposition, **to** describes a motion toward a place: **to the garden, to the school, to the other side of the forest.** As a preposition, it also identifies a person *to whom* something is directed or given: **to John, to her, to my youngest child.** In addition to these functions, **to** is used as a *particle word* in an infinitive: **to run, to jump, to be.** These two uses—the prepositional use and the infinitive use—must be distinguished.

If **to** is followed by a noun phrase or pronoun, it is being used as a preposition. If it is followed by a verb, it is being used as the particle word of an infinitive:

◆ Prepositions

The horses came running **to** the fence when I called.
Mr. Keller sent a large package **to** them.
She was hurrying **to** the door when she fell.

◆ Infinitives

Don't try **to fool** me with your fancy words.
It's going **to be** more difficult than I first thought.
We need **to perform** the surgery on her immediately.

Another difference of usage occurs with the preposition **out**. When it is followed by a noun phrase or pronoun, it is being used as a preposition, such as **out the door**. This same word can be used as an adverb that describes *where* someone or something is and usually indicates that someone is *not at home* or *not in the office*. Let's look at some example sentences:

◆ Prepositions

Lorraine flew **out** the door and ran to the bus stop.
What did you throw **out** the window?
Gray smoke coiled **out** the chimney.

◆ Adverbs

Were you **out** late last night?
Tom wanted to stay **out** with his friends.
The doctor will be **out** until three P.M.

The opposite of **out**, meaning *not at home* or *not in the office*, is **in**. It means *at home* or *at the office*.

I stayed **in** all day.   *I stayed at home all day.*
Dr. Jones won't be **in** today.   *Dr. Jones won't be in the office today.*

The word **in** is also used as a preposition. In such a case, it is followed by a noun or pronoun.

The little boys played **in** the basement.
Look at Jane. I've always been interested **in** her.

Into, onto, upon

The three prepositions **into**, **onto**, and **upon** are composed of two prepositions written as one word. **Into** indicates that someone or something is moving to the inside of an enclosure. **Onto** indicates that someone or something is located on top of something. **Upon** is a synonym for **on**. Consider these examples:

Karen ran into the tent and lit the lantern.   *She ran to the inside of the tent.*
Doug climbed onto the roof with a hammer.   *He is now located on top of the roof.*
A single acorn fell upon the ground.   *It fell on the ground.*

When any of these three prepositions is written as two separate words, the first part becomes an adverb and the second part is a preposition. For example: **Walk in to your left and follow the signs to our offices.** In this sentence, the adverb tells *where* someone should be—not **out**, but **in**. The preposition tells what direction to go: **to your left.**

Now consider this sentence: **I was never turned on to classical music.** In this sentence, the adverb **on** modifies the verb **turned**; it is not part of the preposition. The prepositional phrase is **to classical music.**

Now look at this sentence: **Climb up onto the roof!** Here the adverb **up** modifies the verb **climb.** Someone is being told in what direction to climb. The prepositional phrase **onto the roof** identifies the place where this person is supposed to climb.

The preposition **upon** is used in a couple pat phrases that do not change their form. For example:

Upon my soul!   *an interjection meaning "I'm so surprised"*
                                        or "I can't believe it"

Once **upon** a time . . .   *the opening phrase of some stories and*
                                        fairy tales

Adjectival and adverbial prepositional phrases

Some prepositional phrases modify nouns or pronouns. They are called *adjective phrases*. Similarly, other prepositional phrases are called *adverb phrases* because they modify verbs, adverbs, or adjectives. Be aware that it is not the preposition that determines whether the phrase is adjectival or adverbial, but rather it is the use of the phrase. The same prepositional phrase could be an adjective phrase or an adverb phrase. For example:

The boy **at the window** looked hungry and cold.	*The phrase* at the window *describes the boy; it is adjectival.*
The boy stood **at the window** and waved.	*The phrase* at the window *describes where he stood; it is adverbial.*

When a prepositional phrase describes a noun or pronoun, it normally stands immediately after the noun or pronoun.

The girl **with the bouquet** beamed with pride.
Do you know the woman **with Mr. Simon**?

When the prepositional phrase tells where, when, how, or to what extent something is done, it is adverbial.

The men stood **on the porch** and chatted **about the weather**.	*where, how*
We will be leaving **for Florida** **on Wednesday**.	*where, when*

Exercise
8·4

Complete the following sentences by finishing each prepositional phrase with an appropriate noun phrase. Use any additional phrases to make good sense.

EXAMPLE: We rarely talked about <u>the problems he had with his wife.</u>

1. I returned to _____ to say good-bye to the children.

2. Why do you get into _____ ?

3. Someone next to _____ tried to steal the old coins.

4. Ms. Snyder had to speak in opposition to _____ .

5. The tourists have to get back to _____ .

6. The kittens jumped onto _____ .

7. The judge made his ruling based upon _____ .

8. The castle was located on top of _____ .

9. A child of _____ sat in a corner weeping.

10. No one among _____ .

Write original sentences containing adverbial prepositional phrases. Use the adverbial cue provided as the signal for the kind of phrase required.

EXAMPLE: where <u>Michael sat</u> **on the sofa** and read.

1. where _____

2. when _____

3. how _____

4. where _____

5. when _____

6. how _____

Pronouns in prepositional phrases

Most prepositions can be followed by pronouns that are the replacements for nouns. For example:

John came with **his friends**.	John came with **them**.
The girls hid behind **the door**.	The girls hid behind **it**.
Never speak about **his illness**.	Never speak about **it**.

However, some prepositional phrases that describe *a location in a place* or *a time period* tend to be replaced not by a preposition and a pronoun but rather by **there** or **then**, respectively. For example:

She spent a lot of time **in the city**.	She spent a lot of time **there**.	*not* in it
Mark was **in Asia** for two years.	Mark was **there** for two years.	*not* in it
Jim will arrive **in the morning**.	Jim will arrive **then**.	*not* in it
Were you at work **on Monday**?	Were you at work **then**?	*not* on it

Prepositional phrases do not normally stand alone. An exception is that in an elliptical response to a statement or question, a prepositional phrase can stand alone if the meaning of the rest of the sentence is understood.

Where did you attend college?	**In** California.
The cat usually sleeps under the bed.	No, **under** the rocking chair.

A few other prepositional phrases can stand alone, especially if they are part of an imperative or an interjection.

On your marks, get set, go!
At once!
On your feet!
For heaven's sake!

The preposition **than** can also be used as a conjunction. When it functions as a conjunction, it is followed by a complete clause:

♦ Preposition

My brother is a bit taller **than me**.
Can Mary really run faster **than John**?

♦ Complete clause

My brother works harder **than I like to work**.
Can Mary really run faster **than John can**?

Exercise
8·6

*Rewrite the following sentences, changing the underlined prepositional phrase ending with a noun to a prepositional phrase ending with the appropriate pronoun. Use **there** or **then** where needed.*

EXAMPLE: Jake sat <u>with his friends</u> in the library.

Jake sat <u>with them in the library.</u>

1. I never had anything to do <u>with such people</u>.

_____

2. Did you have a good time <u>in Mexico</u>?

_____

3. The twins were seated directly <u>behind their parents</u>.

_____

4. We can probably meet <u>at about eleven o'clock</u>.

_____

5. Was that rude remark meant <u>for Thomas and me</u>?

_____

6. We used to have a lot of fun <u>during spring vacation</u>.

_____

7. I am completely opposed to <u>what you call a satisfactory contract</u>.

_____

8. My aunt and uncle built a small house <u>in the Bahamas</u>.

_____

9. We found a map <u>at the bottom of the treasure chest</u>.

_____

10. Is this a portrait <u>of Queen Victoria</u>?

_____

Write original sentences using the phrases provided.

EXAMPLE: from my dentist <u>I received this prescription from my dentist.</u>

1. out on the lawn _____

2. alongside the road _____

3. above the forest _____

4. on the lagoon _____

5. because of you _____

6. than her _____

7. toward the opposite shore _____

8. on to the ledge _____

9. than anyone else _____

10. in front of it _____

Using adjectives

Adjectives are words that modify nouns or pronouns. A variety of adjectival forms must be understood in order for you to write accurately. The most common type is the *descriptive adjective*.

Descriptive adjectives

Precisely as their name suggests, descriptive adjectives describe someone or something. The following list contains high-frequency descriptive adjectives. Consider what they tell about a noun they might modify.

beautiful	funny	kind	short
big	handsome	little	soft
blue	happy	red	tall
evil	hard	sad	ugly

The complete listing of all descriptive adjectives would be much longer. You can probably think of many other words that fit this category.

Predicative and attributive adjectives

Adjectives are used primarily in two different ways: *predicatively* and *attributively*. A predicate adjective is one that follows a linking verb and modifies a noun or pronoun "from a distance"—that is, separated from the noun itself by the verb.

subject + linking verb + predicate adjective

Mr. Price is **handsome**.
My vision seems **blurred**.
That really smells **good**!
It suddenly got **cold**.

Here are some commonly used linking verbs.

act	fall	look	smell
appear	feel	prove	sound
become	get	remain	taste
come	grow	seem	

Naturally, adjectives can be modified by any variety of adverbs. For example:

Mr. Price is **very** handsome.
Today the weather became **quite** terrible.

Attributive adjectives, on the other hand, stand before a noun. It is common to use more than one adjective to modify nouns in this position.

attributive adjective + subject + verb

The **young** officer came up to me.
The **frightened young** officer came up to me.
An **old** man sat down to rest.
A **tired old** man sat down to rest.

You can view attributive adjectives as replacements for relative clauses that contain the linking verb **to be**. Compare the following two sentences with the previous two examples:

The officer, **who was** frightened and young, came up to me.
A man, **who was** tired and old, sat down to rest.

Let's look at an example of how a relative clause is changed to become an attributive adjective. Here's the original sentence, with the relative clause set off by commas:

The story, **which is** silly, amused the children.

To convert this sentence, the adjective **silly** is removed from the relative clause. The remaining words in the relative clause are omitted (as are the commas), and the adjective is placed before the noun. The result is a sentence with an attributive adjective, and that sentence conveys the same meaning as the sentence in which there was a relative clause:

The **silly** story amused the children.

When a noun follows a linking verb, it is called a *predicate nominative*. The predicate nominative is a noun that further describes the subject of the sentence. Adjectives can modify the subject, the predicate nominative, or both. For example:

The winner was a man from Holland.
The **eventual** winner was a man from Holland.
The winner was an **athletic** man from Holland.
The **eventual** winner was an **athletic** man from Holland.

A sentence with a predicate nominative can be changed by reversing the positions of the subject and the predicate nominative and *still make complete sense*. This can occur only with linking verbs.

An **athletic** man from Holland was the **eventual** winner.

Some adjectives can be used only as predicate adjectives. They sound awkward if used attributively. Some of the most commonly used ones are these:

afraid	glad	safe
alive	ill	sorry (meaning *apologetic*)
alone	likely	sure
apart	ready	unable
aware		

Let's look at a couple of sentences illustrating correct versus incorrect usage:

The boy was quite **alone**.	*correct usage*
The **alone** boy waited in the hall.	*incorrect usage*

Certain other adjectives should be used only as attributive adjectives. If they are used as predicate adjectives, they should be followed by predicate nominatives.

atomic	north/south
east/west	northern/southern
eastern/western	northern/western
indoor/outdoor	supplementary
maximum	woolen
nationwide	

If **indoor** and **outdoor** are used predicatively, they take the adverbial form **indoors** and **out-doors**. If **supplementary** is used predicatively, its form changes to a noun: **a supplement**. In the case of **woolen**, when used predicatively, it becomes the phrase **made of wool**.

Let's again look at a pair of sentences illustrating correct usage versus incorrect usage:

An **occasional** rain kept the streets wet and slick.	*correct usage*
The rain today was only **occasional**.	*incorrect usage*

Exercise
9·1

Complete each sentence that follows with an appropriate predicate adjective. Then, write a sentence using the same adjective attributively.

EXAMPLE: Mark was very <u>sad</u>.

The <u>sad</u> look in her eyes brought me to tears.

1. a. Are the boys _____ again?

   b. _____

2. a. Grandma's kitchen smelled _____.

   b. _____

3. a. How long has this woman been _____?

   b. _____

4. a. Your report is _____.

   b. _____

5. a. Your new tie looks _____.

   b. _____

6. a. Professor Garcia seemed _____ yesterday.

   b. _____

7. a. Were you _____ as a child?

   b. _____

8. a. The young lawyer seemed rather _____.

   b. _____

9. a. Your rose garden smells _____ !

   b. _____

10. a. Why does her voice sound so _____ ?

   b. _____

Limiting adjectives

There are nine types of limiting adjectives: definite and indefinite articles, possessive adjectives, demonstrative adjectives, indefinite adjectives, interrogative adjectives, cardinal adjectives, ordinal adjectives, proper adjectives, and nouns used as adjectives. The obvious function of any limiting adjective is to limit or to specify some aspect of the noun it modifies.

Definite and indefinite articles

The definite and indefinite articles illustrate this limitation function well. The definite article (**the**) specifies *someone or something as already known or mentioned*. Indefinite articles (**a, an**) identify *an unknown person or thing* and *persons or things in general*. For example:

The man on the corner is my friend.	*A specific man is the topic here. He is known to the speaker.*
A man on the corner was hit by a car.	*An unspecified man is the topic here. He is unknown to the speaker.*
The heavy suitcase belongs to Mary.	*A specific suitcase is the topic here. The speaker knows that it is heavy.*
A heavy suitcase is not allowed.	*Heavy suitcases in general are the topic here.*

Indefinite articles are not used with plural nouns. The complete omission of an article with a plural noun indicates that the meaning is *indefinite*. Compare the following pairs of sentences:

Singular	Plural
The boy plays chess.	**The** boys play chess.
A good student must behave.	Good students must behave.

Possessive adjectives

Possessive adjectives limit the nouns they modify in terms of the ownership implied: **my**, **your**, **his**, **her**, **its**, **our**, and **their**. The possessive **whose**, which inquires into ownership, is also an interrogative adjective but belongs in this group, as well.

My new car is a Ford.	*Ownership of the car is limited to me.*
Her kitten became quite ill.	*Ownership of the kitten is limited to her.*
Our garden did well this year.	*Ownership of the garden is limited to us.*

Demonstrative adjectives

The demonstrative adjectives—**this**, **that**, **these**, and **those**—limit the modified noun to the one identified by the speaker: **this one**, **that one**. The demonstrative adjectives show *closeness* (**this**, **these**) or *distance* (**that**, **those**) in the same way as the demonstrative pronouns.

> **This** book is hard to understand.
> **That** remark was uncalled for.
> **These** men need a job.
> Do you know **those** people?

Exercise
9·2

Write three original sentences containing the noun or phrase provided. Use a definite article or an indefinite article (or both) in the first sentence; use a possessive adjective in the second sentence; and use a demonstrative adjective in the third. If a question mark (?) is also provided, make at least one of your sentences a question.

EXAMPLE: jacket ?

The jacket on the bed belongs to him.

Have you seen my jacket?

This jacket is just what I've been looking for.

1. CD player ?

   a. _____

   b. _____

   c. _____

2. young children

   a. _____

   b. _____

   c. _____

3. yacht ?

   a. _____

   b. _____

   c. _____

4. new lobby

   a. _____

   b. _____

   c. _____

5. pillows ?

  a. _____

  b. _____

  c. _____

6. friends and relatives

  a. _____

  b. _____

  c. _____

7. grammar

  a. _____

  b. _____

  c. _____

8. mathematical formula ?

  a. _____

  b. _____

  c. _____

9. calendar

  a. _____

  b. _____

  c. _____

10. unusual painting

  a. _____

  b. _____

  c. _____

Indefinite adjectives

Indefinite adjectives provide general information about the nouns they modify. They often answer the questions *how much?* or *how many?* Among the most common indefinite adjectives are **all**, **any**, **each**, **every**, **few**, **many**, and **some**. Let's look at some sentences that illustrate their use:

All work must be completed by noon.	*how much work?*
Each candidate will have ten minutes to speak.	*how many candidates?*
Are **some** companies in financial trouble?	*how many companies?*

Interrogative adjectives

The interrogative adjectives are **what**, **which**, and **whose** (as noted earlier, **whose** is also a possessive adjective). They modify nouns in the same way as other limiting adjectives. **What** and **which** inquire into a choice between two persons or things and from among a group of persons or things. **Whose** asks about ownership. Here are some examples:

> **What** airline are you taking to Brazil?
> **What** cities do you want to visit?
> **What** day will you arrive back in the States?
>
> **Which** game do you like best?
> **Which** candidate appeals to you more?
> **Which** dessert did you order?
>
> **Whose** limousine is parked in front of the house?
> **Whose** husband is a famous rap star?
> **Whose** cake won first prize at the fair?

Cardinal adjectives

Cardinal adjectives are simply numbers used as adjectives. They limit the nouns they modify by specifying an amount. That amount can be as little as "zero" or as great as any number you can conceive of. For example:

> **One** boy scraped his knee on the ground.
> **Fifteen** girls are in the contest.
> **Eighty** dollars was too much for the blouse.

Notice that the subject of the last of these sentences is plural, but it is considered a single quantity and therefore takes a singular verb: **Eighty dollars was . . . .** Let's consider the difference between the use of a singular verb and a plural verb with such quantities.

If there are eighty *individual* dollar bills on the floor, you can say: **Eighty dollars are on the floor.** If, instead, you wish to refer to the entire quantity of eighty dollars as a single sum of money, you can say: **Eighty dollars is more than I want to spend.**

Ordinal adjectives

Numbers are used in a slightly different adjectival form with ordinal adjectives. These adjectives limit the nouns they modify by specifying numerical order. For example:

> The **first** question on the test was simple.
> They're celebrating their **fiftieth** wedding anniversary.
> Jake is the **twelfth** boy in line.

The majority of ordinal adjectives are formed by adding **-th** to the end of a number: **fourth**, **thirtieth**, **hundredth**, and so on. There are only a few irregular forms, as follows:

CARDINAL NUMBER	ORDINAL NUMBER
one	first
two	second
three	third
five	fifth

Write an original sentence for each of the cue phrases provided.

1. each student _____

2. some residents _____

3. his first attempt _____

4. every third day _____

5. eleven players _____

6. many complaints _____

7. few demands _____

8. our daughter _____

9. the fifth row _____

10. too much noise _____

*Using each cue phrase provided, write a question with **what** as an interrogative adjective. Then write a response to your question.*

EXAMPLE: color

What color is Jim's new suit?

Jim's new suit is bright green.

1. wristwatch

   a. _____

   b. _____

2. blanket

   a. _____

   b. _____

3. set of towels

   a. _____

   b. _____

4. length

   a. _____

   b. _____

*Follow the same directions, but write your questions with **which** as an interrogative adjective.*

5. writing implements

   a. _____

   b. _____

6. path

   a. _____

   b. _____

7. breakfast menu

   a. _____

   b. _____

*Follow the same directions, but write your questions with **whose** as an interrogative adjective.*

8. passport and visa

   a. _____

   b. _____

9. Cuban relatives

   a. _____

   b. _____

10. coin purse

   a. _____

   b. _____

Proper adjectives and nouns used as adjectives

Proper adjectives are words that are proper nouns but act as modifiers of other nouns. Since proper nouns are capitalized, capitalization is also required when they are used as adjectives. A large category of proper adjectives comprises words that come from country or language names and that can be used both attributively and predicatively. Here are some examples:

> I love **Italian** food.
> Is **French** champagne the best?
> He said the **American** cars are less expensive.
> I believe this drawing is **Japanese**.

The same need for capitalization applies to proper names; however, proper names tend to be used only attributively. For example:

> We read a **Shakespearean** play.
> The **Hilton** mansion is hidden by trees.
> The **Bush** administration ended in 2009.
> Isn't that a **Streisand** song?

Many other nouns can also act as modifiers. If they are not proper nouns, they do not need to be capitalized and can be used only attributively. For example:

> Several **party** gifts were identical.
> The **wedding** guests were starting to get tipsy.
> I think I lost my **credit** card.

Exercise 9·5

Using the noun cues provided, write original sentences with the nouns functioning as adjectives.

EXAMPLE: Ford <u>There's a Ford dealership over there.</u>

1. Elizabethan _____

2. divorce _____

3. Kennedy _____

4. recreation _____

5. chemistry _____

6. faculty _____

7. White House _____

8. movie _____

9. baseball _____

10. Jack London _____

Infinitives

In some cases, an infinitive can function as an adjective. The infinitive usually immediately follows the noun or pronoun it modifies. For example:

> This is always a fun show **to watch**.
> We still haven't found anyone **to hire** for this position.
> Professor Keller's class would be a great one **to take**.

Complete each sentence that follows with any appropriate infinitive.

EXAMPLE: This is a difficult book <u>to read</u>.

1. We have several new plants _____ .

2. Do you have any new music _____ ?

3. This is really something _____ .

4. Do you have any money _____ ?

5. Maria still has several letters _____ .

Using the infinitives that follow as adjectives, write original sentences.

6. to develop _____

7. to clean up _____

8. to grade _____

9. to defend _____

10. to be praised _____

Using adverbs

Adverbs modify verbs, adjectives, or other adverbs. They can be individual words, phrases, or clauses.

> adverb + verb
> adverb + adjective
> adverb + adverb

Adverb types and forms

There is more than one type of adverb. This chapter provides you with information on adverbs of manner, time, frequency, degree, and place, as well as adverbs that provide a comment on a situation.

Individual adverbs are formed simply by adding the suffix **-ly** to an adjective. Naturally, the English rules of spelling apply; for example, a final *y* is changed to *i* when an adverb is formed (**happy** → **happily**). Let's look at some example adjectives and their adverbial formation:

ADJECTIVE	ADVERB
careful	carefully
quick	quickly
simple	simply

A few adverbs are identical to their adjectival counterparts. For example:

ADJECTIVE	ADVERB
early	early
fast	fast
late	late

Adjectives that describe certain increments of time *look like adverbs* but are true adjectives. For example:

> We're paid on an **hourly** basis.
> I take a **daily** vitamin supplement.
> Grandma has a **weekly** appointment with her doctor.

> Your **monthly** salary is going to be increased.
> My **yearly** physical exam always makes me nervous.

Still other adjectives that look like adverbs are not related to the ones that describe increments of time. Examples are **deadly**, **early**, **lively**, and **only**.

When an adverb is used in the comparative or superlative, the suffix **-ly** is generally not added. However, if the comparative and superlative are formed with **more** and **most**, the suffix **-ly** is added.

POSITIVE	COMPARATIVE	SUPERLATIVE
quickly	quicker	(the) quickest
softly	softer	(the) softest
well	better	(the) best
awkwardly	more awkwardly	most awkwardly
beautifully	more beautifully	most beautifully
carefully	more carefully	most carefully

Don't confuse **late** with **lately**. Both are adverbs, but they have different meanings.

The girls arrived **late**.	*the opposite of* early
He's been rather moody **lately**.	*recently*

Adverbs of manner

Adverbs of manner form a large category. They tell *how* something is done. Consider the following sentences:

Martin drove **slowly**.	*How did he drive? Slowly.*
I **carefully** removed the battery.	*How did I remove the battery? Carefully.*
She kissed the baby **gently**.	*How did she kiss the baby? Gently.*

Adverbs of manner can be individual words or phrases. Let's look at some of these:

INDIVIDUAL WORDS	PHRASES
badly	in anger
politely	with a sly grin
sarcastically	with great sadness

Adverbs of manner tend to follow the predicate of a sentence.

subject + predicate + adverb of manner

Bill + spoke to her + angrily.
The team played **badly**.
He tried to speak **politely**.
She gave them the news **with great sadness**.
Tom began to shout **in anger**.

Adverbs of time

Adverbs such as **now**, **still**, **yesterday**, **just**, **finally**, and **Sunday** tell *when* something occurred. These adverbs of time are part of a category that includes individual words, phrases, and clauses. For example:

INDIVIDUAL WORDS	PHRASES	CLAUSES
finally	during the exam	after the game ended
recently	in the spring	I got on the bus
today	on Monday before	since she arrived here

Adverbs of time can introduce a sentence or follow it.

subject + predicate + adverb of time

He + left for work + at seven.

adverb of time + subject + predicate

At seven + he + left for work.
Recently, I bought a new laptop.
I bought a new laptop **recently**.

During the exam, Tina began to feel ill.
Tina began to feel ill **during the exam**.

Before I got on the bus, I realized I had lost my ticket.
I realized I had lost my ticket **before I got on the bus**.

Exercise
10·1

Using each set of words and phrases provided, write a sentence with the adverb of manner in the appropriate position.

EXAMPLE: men / drive / carefully / mountains
             The men had to drive carefully through the mountains.

1. children / run / school / with joy

   _____

2. baritone / sing / better / soprano

   _____

3. brother / lounge / lazily / sofa / TV

   _____

4. Michael / show / car / with great pride

   _____

5. she / act / responsibly / accident

   _____

6. woman / mutter / weakly / that / ill

   _____

7. professor / congratulate / with a bit of sarcasm

   _____

8. eight-year-old / play / beautifully

   _____

9. little James / recite / capably / bow

   _____

10. Ellen / slap / with rage

   _____

Using each adverb of time provided, write two original sentences: one in which the adverb introduces the action, and one in which it follows it.

EXAMPLE: recently

Recently, I found an old picture of Dad.

I found an old picture of Dad recently.

1. during the storm

   a. _____

   b. _____

2. yesterday

   a. _____

   b. _____

3. on the weekend

   a. _____

   b. _____

4. soon

   a. _____

   b. _____

5. next Friday

   a. _____

   b. _____

6. in time

   a. _____

   b. _____

7. after Paul gets here

   a. _____

   b. _____

8. in June

   a. _____

   b. _____

9. last year

   a. _____

   b. _____

10. before I studied English

a. _____

b. _____

Adverbs of frequency

Adverbs of frequency tell *how often* something occurs. They can be individual words or phrases. For example:

INDIVIDUAL WORDS	PHRASES
never	at times
sometimes	in the rarest of moments
usually	with great frequency

When an adverb of frequency is an individual word, it tends to stand just before the verb. If it is a phrase, it usually can either introduce the sentence or follow it. Let's look at some example sentences:

We **rarely** stay out very late.
My sister **often** invites her friends over to listen to music.

At times, I just want to drop everything and go out.
Mr. Johnson showed up at our door **with great regularity**.

Adverbs of degree

Adverbs of degree tell *to what extent* something is done. Some of the most commonly used adverbs of degree are listed here:

adequately	perfectly
almost	practically
entirely	profoundly
extremely	really
greatly	strongly
highly	totally
hugely	tremendously
immensely	very
moderately	virtually
partially	

The adverbs in this category are used to modify verbs, adjectives, or other adverbs. The position of the adverb in a sentence is determined by the word it modifies:

◆ Verbs

The children enjoyed the circus **immensely**.
The lawyer **strongly** advocated suing the company.

◆ Adjectives

She was an **extremely** beautiful woman.
Bill had become **profoundly** depressed.

♦ Adverbs

They sang **really** badly.
The project was progressing **moderately** well.

Rewrite the following sentences with an appropriate adverb of frequency.

EXAMPLE: She spoke with John.

<u>She never spoke with John.</u>

1. We supported our troops fighting overseas.

   _____

2. Larry had to work on the weekend.

   _____

3. I planned to take art courses at the college.

   _____

4. Do you work at the new plant in the suburbs?

   _____

5. Martin renews his subscription to this magazine.

   _____

6. We drink coffee with breakfast.

   _____

7. Did your parents live in Europe?

   _____

8. My sister and I baked a cake or cookies.

   _____

9. Jim and Ellen went to a dance.

   _____

10. Have you thought of becoming a doctor?

   _____

Write an original sentence using each adverb of degree and the accompanying verb, adjective, or adverb provided.

EXAMPLE: very strong <u>My cousin Jake is a very strong man.</u>

1. highly emotional _____

2. totally irrelevant _____

3. recommend highly _____

4. immensely proudly _____

5. hugely successful _____

6. weep profoundly _____

7. really stubbornly _____

8. really stubborn _____

9. entirely false _____

10. partially true _____

Adverbs of place

Adverbs of place tell *where* an action occurs. Some of these adverbs are single words. For example:

abroad	inside
anywhere	somewhere
downstairs	there
here	underground

Other adverbs of place appear in phrase form, particularly in prepositional phrases.

alongside the road	next door
at home	on the hearth
in the bedroom	over there

Let's look at some example sentences:

They lived **abroad** for five years.
They were working **somewhere** on a secret project.

Jack was making up the bed **in the bedroom**.
We spend a lot of time **at home**.

Using each of the adverb cues provided once, write two original sentences.

EXAMPLE: here / in the garden

They stopped here for a bite to eat.

Dad wanted to take a nap in the garden.

1. there / on the roof

   a. _____

   b. _____

2. outside / next door

   a. _____

   b. _____

3. anywhere / over the mantle

   a. _____

   b. _____

4. upstairs / in a small box

   a. _____

   b. _____

5. underground / beyond the river

   a. _____

   b. _____

6. somewhere / under a leafy tree

   a. _____

   b. _____

Adverbs that make a comment

Some adverbs make a comment on a situation. They identify the speaker's or writer's *viewpoint* or *opinion* on the subject matter of a sentence. Some commonly used comment or viewpoint adverbs follow:

bravely	presumably
carelessly	seriously
certainly	simply
clearly	stupidly

cleverly	surely
confidentially	technically
definitely	theoretically
disappointingly	thoughtfully
foolishly	truthfully
generously	unbelievably
happily	undoubtedly
kindly	(un)fortunately
naturally	(un)luckily
obviously	wisely
personally	wrongly

When adverbs of this category are used in context, they show the degree to which the speaker or writer agrees or disagrees with a statement. These adverbs can also show disapproval or skepticism. Let's look at some example sentences:

She **clearly** has no understanding of the topic.	*The speaker has doubts about her understanding.*
Theoretically, the project should be completed by May.	*The speaker is skeptical that the completion date can be met.*
Wisely, he chose to drop out of the competition.	*The speaker believes the decision to drop out was a good one.*

Some adverbs of this type are placed only at the beginning of the sentence. For example:

Confidentially, I think that Martha is being dishonest.
Presumably, the storm is going to let up and we'll be able to leave.
Happily, the child was found unharmed.

Certain of these adverbs can either introduce the sentence or follow the subject. For example:

Naturally, I thought I had done the right thing.
I **naturally** thought I had done the right thing.

Certainly, Jean understands why you can't go tonight.
Jean **certainly** understands why you can't go tonight.

Personally, I believe the election came off quite smoothly.
I **personally** believe that the election came off quite smoothly.

Be careful with the adverb **happily**. It is both an adverb of manner and an adverb of viewpoint or comment. If it tells *how* something is done, it is an adverb of manner.

Tina spoke **happily** about her engagement.

If it expresses a point of view, suggesting that the subject matter of the sentence is good news, then the adverb is one of viewpoint or comment.

Happily, the man found his wallet and could buy the tickets.

Rewrite each of the following sentences twice: first placing the adverb provided in parentheses at the beginning of the sentence, and then placing it after the subject.

EXAMPLE: (obviously) The blizzard is worse than expected.

Obviously, the blizzard is worse than expected.

The blizzard obviously is worse than expected.

1. (surely) You don't believe his story.

    a. _____

    b. _____

2. (undoubtedly) The man is a genius.

    a. _____

    b. _____

3. (personally) I feel I can place my trust in this woman.

    a. _____

    b. _____

4. (presumably) Mr. Lee has a wonderful new job in Boston.

    a. _____

    b. _____

5. (cleverly) Daniel found a seat next to the pretty girl from Korea.

    a. _____

    b. _____

Adverb placement in a sentence

Adverbs tend to be placed in a specific position in a sentence. This is merely a tendency, however, and some adverbs are more flexible and make sense in more than one position. In some cases, the position of an adverb in a sentence is determined by what element is stressed or by the actual function of the adverb. Also, some adverbs can be used in more than one way. For example:

Disappointingly, Mark received another bad grade.	*adverb of viewpoint introducing the sentence*
Bill **disappointingly** missed making a goal.	*adverb of viewpoint following the subject*
She gave a **disappointingly** weak response.	*adverb of degree modifying an adjective*

Following are some general rules for determining adverb placement in a sentence:

◆ Adverbs of manner, adverbs of time, and adverbs of place stand after the verb or the predicative expression at the end of the sentence.

subject + verb + manner/time/place

The boys stared **glumly** at the scoreboard.   *adverb of manner*
They'll arrive in town **next week**.   *adverb of time*
Phillip stood **near the door**.   *adverb of place*

◆ Adverbs of frequency are placed before the main verb in a sentence.

subject + frequency + verb

Jack **often** visits us when he's in town.
She **rarely** spoke of life in her village.

An exception is that if the sentence contains an auxiliary verb, an adverb of frequency usually follows that auxiliary.

Maria has **never** been to Canada.
My dad will **usually** cry at a sad movie.
You should **regularly** floss your teeth.

Also, if the verb **to be** is used as the main verb of a clause, an adverb of frequency will follow that verb.

She was **seldom** in class.
You are **always** the best musician in the orchestra.

◆ Adverbs of degree follow the verb or verb phrase they modify—but if they modify an adjective or another adverb, they are placed before them.

The good news about Dad's health pleased   *modified verb*
   them **tremendously**.
He had a **profoundly** infected wound.   *modified adjective*
They had to drive **really** slowly.   *modified adverb*

◆ Adverbs of viewpoint or comment commonly begin the sentence—though, some can follow the subject. For example:

viewpoint + subject + verb

Wisely, they left the stalled car and walked to town.
Undoubtedly, you have no confidence in yourself.

subject + viewpoint + verb

She **clearly** has no intention of paying me back.
Bob **obviously** overslept again.

The explanations of adverb placement in this chapter have been qualified by words such as *commonly used* or *tendency*, because there can be exceptions to the rules. The rules are not finite.

One frequent exception to the rules is the placement of an adverb at the beginning of a sentence, rather than in its normal position, for emphasis. For example:

Now you finally come up with an answer to my question!
Rarely do I ever watch such television programs!
Sometimes I think about my days back on the farm.

Write original sentences using both of the adverb cues provided. Note that one adverb in each pair is an adverb of viewpoint or comment, while the other is of another type.

EXAMPLE: confidentially / really <u>Confidentially, I think that's a really poor idea.</u>

1. clearly / usually _____

2. foolishly / last week _____

3. bravely / very _____

4. fortunately / sometimes _____

5. personally / really _____

Rewrite each sentence that follows three times, using the three adverbs provided in parentheses in their appropriate positions.

EXAMPLE: She bought a pretty sweater. (naturally / on Monday / really)

<u>Naturally, she bought a pretty sweater.</u>

<u>She bought a pretty sweater on Monday.</u>

<u>She bought a really pretty sweater.</u>

6. I ran to the window and saw Bill. (quickly / fortunately / suddenly)

a. _____

b. _____

c. _____

7. Juanita destroyed the strange object. (wisely / immediately / very)

a. _____

b. _____

c. _____

8. They carried her into the living room. (after she fainted / carefully / around five o'clock)

a. _____

b. _____

c. _____

9. The old men sat around the little table. (presumably / extremely / silently)

a. _____

b. _____

c. _____

10. Her left leg is broken. (seriously / once again / in two places)

a. _____

b. _____

c. _____

Present and past participles

11

There are two types of participles: *present participles* and *past participles*. Both types can be used as modifiers.

Present participles

A present participle is formed by adding **-ing** to the infinitive of a verb while dropping the particle word **to**:

> to go → going
> to help → helping
> to be → being
> to develop → developing

Although present participles are used attributively, they have a special characteristic: they can modify a noun by standing either before it or after it. If the present participle stands after the noun, it is in a sense an elliptical relative clause. Here is an illustration:

The **weeping** girl was Tim's sister	
The girl **weeping** was Tim's sister.	*The girl who was weeping was Tim's sister.*
The **spinning** top made me dizzy.	
The top **spinning** made me dizzy.	*The top that was spinning made me dizzy.*
The **running** boys were scared.	
The boys **running** were scared.	*The boys who were running were scared.*

Present participles can also introduce a phrase that modifies a noun or pronoun in a sentence. For example:

> **Running down the hill**, Jim tripped and sprained his ankle.
> **Sitting alone in the dark**, she suddenly had a feeling of dread.

Phrases or clauses that modify the noun or pronoun they precede can indicate a new tense or a modified meaning by use of an auxiliary. Let's look at some examples:

Being accused of a crime, Jim was forced   *present passive*
    to be interrogated.
Having been invited to the party, Juan   *past passive*
    went out to buy a new suit.
Being able to sing well, Nancy was asked   *modal auxiliary*
    to join the choir.

Present participles cannot be used predicatively, but they can be used *to modify a noun in the predicate*. Present participles in a predicate can stand before the noun they modify or after the noun they modify, and the verb in the sentence can be either a linking verb or a transitive verb. In both usages, they are replacements for relative clauses.

First let's look at some examples of present participles that stand before the noun they modify in the predicate:

This is a **developing** story.   *story that is developing*
The woman observed the slowly **moving**   *caravan that is moving slowly*
    caravan.
That was a **frightening** experience!   *experience that was frightening*

With the phrase **there is/there are**, the modifying present participle stands after the noun. The phrase **there is/there are** can be in any tense. For example:

There really was no story **developing**.   *story that was developing*
There is a storm **brewing**.   *storm that is brewing*
There will be three trained bears **dancing**.   *bears that will be dancing*

When the verb in the sentence is transitive, this same position following the noun is possible for a present participle.

They were recording the professor **speaking**.
The doctor watched her eyes rapidly **blinking**.
I felt my heart **beating** wildly in my chest.

Exercise
11·1

Fill in each blank with an appropriate present-participle modifier.

EXAMPLE: The <u>pouting</u> boy had just been punished.

1. _____ hyenas are native to Africa.

2. My parents want a new _____ table.

3. All night long, I listened to the old clock _____ .

4. She said nothing _____ .

5. The boys _____ over the soccer ball are bullies.

6. _____ , my uncle collected a variety of artworks.

7. What a large _____ vessel!

8. _____ clouds moved swiftly overhead.

9. There won't be another train _____ soon.

10. There were numerous rumors _____ .

Past participles

Past participles can be used as adjectives and are in the same verbal form as the perfect tenses, but the auxiliary **have** is omitted.

> to break → broken
> to write → written
> to arrest → arrested
> to deliver → delivered

In many cases, past participles—just like present participles—can modify a noun by standing before it or after it. When it stands after the noun, the past participle is like an elliptical relative clause, but the verb in that clause is in the passive voice. Let's look at some examples:

The **arrested** man tried to flee.	
The man **arrested** tried to flee.	*The man who was arrested tried to flee.*
The **stolen** money was retrieved.	
The money **stolen** was retrieved.	*The money that was stolen was retrieved.*
The **burned** books were in Latin.	
The books **burned** were in Latin.	*The books that were burned were in Latin.*

Past participles can also introduce a phrase that modifies a noun or pronoun in a sentence. For example:

> **Discovered in southern Mexico**, the village had apparently been abandoned years ago.
> **Shaken by the clap of thunder**, they left the tent and went in the house.

In contrast to present participles, past participles can be used as predicative adjectives after linking verbs.

> The clock was **broken**, so Tim placed it in a box in the attic.
> Their vacation plans were **ruined**.
> His voice finally sounded **rested**.

This usage, which often resembles the passive voice, is further addressed in Chapter 17, which discusses the passive voice in detail.

Past participles can also be used *to modify a noun in the predicate*. Past participles in the predicate can stand before the noun they modify or after the noun they modify, and the verb in the sentence can be either a linking verb or a transitive verb. In both usages, they are replacements for relative clauses.

First let's look at some examples of past participles that stand before the noun they modify:

The athlete has a well-**developed** body.	*body that was well developed*
This is a **completed** version of the story.	*version that was completed*
Her **frightened** face told me everything.	*face that was frightened*

With the phrase **there is/there are**, the modifying past participle stands after the noun. The phrase **there is/there are** can be used in any tense. For example:

> There was a message **stuffed** in his pocket.
> Will there be new invitations **sent** out?
> At that tragic moment, there wasn't a single word **spoken**.

Exercise 11·2

Fill in each blank with an appropriate past-participle modifier.

EXAMPLE: Each <u>written</u> exercise is worth ten points.

1. _____ documents are of no help.

2. _____ , the little boy ran up the stairs and jumped in bed..

3. _____ , James turned away and began to sob.

4. I think the meat loaf smells _____ .

5. Who took the _____ garments from this room?

6. I have the valley _____ on this map.

7. _____ , Susan let out a little shriek and then smiled in embarrassment.

8. A _____ pot never boils. (proverb)

9. Where is the little boy _____ alone in the park?

10. This is the manuscript _____ in that old chest.

Exercise 11·3

Using each verb cue provided, write two original sentences: one with the verb cue written as a present participle, and one with the verb cue written as a past participle.

EXAMPLE: read

This reading material is meant for adults.

The previously read statement is full of exaggerations.

1. write

a. _____

b. _____

2. break

a. _____

b. _____

3. charge

a. _____

b. _____

4. leak

a. _____

b. _____

Follow the same directions, but write one original sentence with an introductory phrase that modifies a noun or pronoun and is introduced by a present participle.

EXAMPLE: follow

Following the paths of the maze, the man became disoriented.

5. lie

_____

6. hope

_____

7. drive

_____

Follow the same directions, but write one original sentence with an introductory phrase that modifies a noun or pronoun and is introduced by a past participle.

EXAMPLE: develop

Developed for the space program, this ceramic is now in public use.

8. place

_____

9. beat

_____

10. drive

_____

Adverbs and participles

Since participles can be used as adjectives, and adjectives can be modified by adverbs, it is logical that adverbs can modify participles. This is true of both present and past participles. However, because participles are derived from verbs, only those adverbs that can modify a verb can also modify a participle. Let's look at a few examples with present participles:

He speaks **slowly**.	I listened to the man speaking **slowly**.
The satellite orbits **regularly**.	They observed the **regularly** orbiting satellite.
She stared **coldly** at him.	The woman staring **coldly** at him was Jane.

Adverbs modify past participles in a similar manner, but the verb that becomes a past-participle modifier is in the passive voice. For example:

The boy was **rarely** punished.	The **rarely** punished boy was arrogant.
The words had been **neatly** printed.	The **neatly** printed words were addressed to Santa.
It was calculated **properly**.	He showed the figures calculated **properly**.

Since adverbs can be prepositional phrases, prepositional phrases can also modify present and past participles used as modifiers. This occurs most frequently when the adverb modifier follows the noun or pronoun it modifies.

The man standing **near the door** isn't one of our guests.
Some **qualified for the job** were a bit too young.

11·4

Add an appropriate adverb that modifies the present or past participle in each phrase that follows.

EXAMPLE: the <u>slowly</u> spinning top; a window shattered <u>in the storm</u>

1. the _____ grazing cattle

2. the _____ twirling dancers

3. someone behaving _____

4. a shed leaning _____ to one side

5. the _____ beaming parents

6. a _____ tuned instrument

7. the _____ copied text

8. a chair propped _____

9. the _____ mixed paint

10. song _____ sung

Exercise

11·5

Write original sentences using the following participles and phrases as modifiers.

EXAMPLE: running along the bank of the river
Running along the bank of the river, Tim slipped and fell in the water.

1. fully rested

_____

2. giggling

_____

3. merrily strumming on an old banjo

_____

108 PRACTICE MAKES PERFECT English Sentence Builder

4. having been voted president

_____

5. collected over the years

_____

6. suggested by a professor

_____

7. sputtering nervously

_____

8. driven to madness

_____

9. having to remain at home

_____

10. vigorously bubbling

_____

 # Using infinitives

In order to write effectively in English, it is necessary to understand some important verb forms. One of them is the infinitive.

Verbs that combine with infinitives

Infinitives are considered the *base form* of a verb. They are composed of the verb and the particle word **to**: **to look**, **to run**, **to see**, and so on. When used as verbs, infinitives can follow certain auxiliaries.

> **auxiliary + infinitive**
>
> to be able + to see

For example:

> I am supposed **to be** home by ten.
> You ought **to hurry.**
> She has **to wait.**

Also, certain other words often require an infinitive usage after them and sometimes are preceded by a noun or pronoun object. Some of the most commonly used ones are listed here:

agree	fail	prepare
appear	forget	pretend
ask	hesitate	promise
beg	hope	refuse
care	learn	regret
claim	manage	remember

Let's look at their use in a few example sentences:

> She **agreed to work** on a solution with me.
> I **hesitate to think** about what might happen.
> Did you **ask** Tim **to sign up** for the same class?

Functions of an infinitive

When an infinitive is used as a *verbal*, it is functioning not as a verb but as a different part of speech. Infinitives can be used as *nouns*, *adjectives*, and *adverbs*.

When an infinitive is used as a noun, it occurs in some of the structures of all other nouns: *the subject of a sentence, the direct object of a sentence, a predicate nominative, the object of a preposition, an appositive,* and *a modifier.*

Subject of a sentence

Let's look at some infinitives used as subjects. Note that infinitives as subjects can be part of a phrase.

> **subject infinitive + verb + complement**
>
> **To study in Europe** is a dream of mine.
> **To become a leader** was her greatest ambition.
> **To learn a foreign language** is part of a good education.
> Her final wish was **to see her grandson graduate from college**.

Exercise

12·1

Complete each sentence that follows by filling in the blank with an appropriate phrase for the infinitive provided.

EXAMPLE: To work <u>for this company</u> is really a privilege.

1. To prepare _____ will take a long time.

2. To attend _____ should be your goal.

3. To sleep _____ will not be tolerated.

4. To play _____ is just a dream of hers.

5. To die _____ was the young warrior's wish.

6. To camp _____ gave us a lot of pleasure.

7. To serve _____ became his destiny.

8. To develop _____ has been a difficult task.

9. To climb _____ had become her obsession.

10. To write _____ is not as easy as it sounds.

Direct object of a sentence

Infinitives can appear as direct objects as follows:

> **subject + transitive verb + direct object infinitive**
>
> She loved **to write poetry**.
> I finally arranged **to study abroad**.
> He won't attempt **to climb that mountain** again.

Remember that some auxiliaries are followed by an infinitive that does not include the particle word **to**. For example: **He must run. They can sing.** Following the verb **to help**, the same thing occurs with infinitives that are used as direct objects. Let's look at an example:

Can you help lift the sofa?   *Can you help **to** lift the sofa?*

Complete each sentence by filling in the blank with an appropriate phrase following the infinitive provided as a direct object.

EXAMPLE: John hated to waste <u>time at the mall</u>.

1. Do you want to wait _____ ?

2. The girls attempted to hide _____ .

3. Mark often forgot to lock _____ .

4. Please help me find _____ .

5. Jake wanted to paint _____ .

Now complete each of the following sentences with an original infinitive phrase.

6. Jim and Jerry helped me _____ .

7. I really need _____ .

8. The young girl pretended _____ ?

9. Don't try _____ .

10. Did you remember _____ ?

Complete each of the following sentences appropriately, using the infinitive phrase provided as the subject of the sentence.

EXAMPLE: To play the piano <u>is a goal of mine</u>.

1. To live a clean and honorable life _____ .

2. To visit Rome _____ .

3. To become rich _____ .

4. To repair racing cars _____ .

5. To travel into space _____ .

6. To study physics in Japan _____ .

7. To end pollution _____ .

8. To become a citizen _____ .

9. To earn my degree _____ .

10. To see my mother healthy again _____ .

Passive-voice infinitives can be used in the same way as other infinitives. For example:

>**To be elected** to high office was her goal.
>John's only wish is **to be respected** by his peers.

Predicate nominative

It's also common for some infinitives to function as a predicate nominative. For instance:

>Her first duty was **to protect her children**.
>My goal is **to be appointed chairman of the committee**.
>Is your purpose here **to ruin this project or to help improve it**?

Object of a preposition

Likewise, infinitive phrases can sometimes be the object of a preposition. For instance:

>I want nothing but **to see my children happy**.
>Barry learned nothing in the class except **to cheat**.

Appositive

When an infinitive phrase is used as an appositive, it can appear in either one of two positions in a sentence: immediately after the word or phrase that it explains or describes, or at the end of a sentence that begins with an impersonal **it**. Here are examples of the first type of apposition:

>My goal, **to study in Mexico**, is about to become a reality.
>Mary's suggestion, **to collect aluminum cans along the road**, was quickly rejected.
>The notion, **to dig a tunnel under the ocean**, is preposterous.

An appositive at the end of a sentence is sometimes called a *delayed appositive*. It is used to describe the impersonal subject of a sentence **it**. For example:

>It hurt me a lot **to see her with another man**.
>It would give us great pleasure **to see you win that prize**.
>It seemed naive **to hope for peace at this time**.

A delayed infinitive can be identified by testing it as the subject of the sentence in place of **it**. If the infinitive subject of the sentence make sense, it is a delayed infinitive.

>**To see her with another man** hurt me a lot.
>**To see you win that prize** would give us great pleasure.
>**To hope for peace at this time** seemed naive.

Using the infinitive phrase provided, write three original sentences: one with the phrase used as a predicate nominative, one with the phrase used as an appositive, and one with the phrase used as a delayed appositive.

EXAMPLE: to visit Alaska

His only desire was to visit Alaska.

Jane's goal, to visit Alaska, would become a reality.

It became impossible to visit Alaska.

1. to marry Jack

   a. _____

   b. _____

   c. _____

2. to become a famous actor

   a. _____

   b. _____

   c. _____

3. to understand grammar better

   a. _____

   b. _____

   c. _____

4. to run in the marathon

   a. _____

   b. _____

   c. _____

5. not to become conceited

   a. _____

   b. _____

   c. _____

6. never to cry

   a. _____

   b. _____

   c. _____

7. to develop great skill playing the guitar

a. _____

b. _____

c. _____

Modifier

Used as modifiers, infinitives can act as both adjectives and adverbs. When an infinitive modifies a noun or pronoun, it is used as an adjective.

Jill is the only girl in our class **to remain single**.   *modifies* girl

Mr. Lee is the one **to see about getting a job here**.   *modifies* one

This is the only road **to take**.   *modifies* road

When an infinitive acts as an adverb, it modifies a verb and usually answers the question *why?* You can test this adverbial usage by adding the phrase **in order to** to the infinitive. If the phrase makes sense, it is used adverbially. Let's look at some example sentences:

Jonathan came **to help with our move into the new apartment**.   *in order to help*

Ms. Smythe phoned **to apologize**.   *in order to apologize*

The applicant is waiting **to see the boss**.   *in order to see the boss*

Exercise
12·5

Complete each of the following sentences with any appropriate infinitive modifier—an adjective for a noun or pronoun, an adverb for a verb.

EXAMPLE: Frank is really a man <u>to be admired</u>.

1. The little boy cried _____.

2. The documents _____ are on my desk.

3. Her parents came along _____.

4. Ms. Garcia is the person _____.

5. The guard gave the signal _____.

6. They decided to stop at a motel _____.

7. We came by way of another street _____.

8. Is there a better way _____?

9. She applied for a job _____.

10. The issue _____ is how we find enough money for a new house.

Write an original sentence using each of the phrases provided.

EXAMPLE: person to watch

The only person to watch is the one with experience.

1. to enjoy the music

_____

2. to be supported

_____

3. to locate

_____

4. to applaud

_____

5. to be contradicted

_____

6. to spell

_____

7. to forgive

_____

8. to be forgiven

_____

9. to eliminate

_____

10. to judge

_____

In the sentences that follow, change the underlined word or phrase to any two appropriate infinitives or infinitive phrases.

EXAMPLE: A study session can be boring.

To read Latin texts can be boring.

To paint a white wall can be boring.

1. She arrived early from work.

   a. _____

   b. _____

2. Her idea, a network of computers, was only slowly accepted.

   a. _____

   b. _____

3. Music gradually became Tom's passion.

   a. _____

   b. _____

4. There was nothing to do but this.

   a. _____

   b. _____

5. My only choice was total capitulation.

   a. _____

   b. _____

 **·13·**

Using gerunds

Another important verbal is the gerund. It is formed just like a present participle: the suffix **-ing** is added to the infinitive, while the particle word **to** is omitted.

> to go → going
> to sing → singing

Present participles, as opposed to gerunds, are used to form the progressive tenses and as modifiers:

- ◆ Progressive tense showing an incomplete action

  > I **am studying** for a big exam.
  > She **was planning** on a vacation to Ireland.

- ◆ Modifier

  > The **swirling** waters meant danger ahead.
  > The man **following us** looked sinister.

Functions of the gerund

Gerunds have a different use in sentences. They act as nouns, and they can be part of any grammatical structure that a noun can: *subject, predicate nominative, object, modifier, possessive, object of a preposition*, or *appositive*.

When a gerund is used as the subject of a sentence, it can be a single word or part of a phrase. For example:

> **Spinning** is a popular exercise at my health club.
> **Working** for the railroad meant job security.

The same is true if the gerund or gerund phrase is in the predicate nominative.

> Jim's passion soon became **singing**.
> Their daily chore was **washing** the dishes after dinner.

Using the phrase provided to form a gerund, write one sentence with the gerund serving as the subject, and then write a second sentence with the same gerund serving as the predicate nominative.

EXAMPLE: to have a party

Having a party can be a lot of work.

Her only thought was having a party for him.

1. to borrow some money

    a. _____

    b. _____

2. to collect stamps

    a. _____

    b. _____

3. to travel around New England

    a. _____

    b. _____

4. to complain

    a. _____

    b. _____

5. to solve her money problems

    a. _____

    b. _____

6. to swear

    a. _____

    b. _____

7. to jog in the park

    a. _____

    b. _____

8. to be on the team

    a. _____

    b. _____

9. to cry

a. _____

b. _____

10. to avoid an accident

a. _____

b. _____

Gerunds can be used as direct objects following many verbs. Just about any verb that can have a noun or pronoun direct object can also have a gerund as its direct object. Let's look at some examples:

Noun object	**Gerund object**
My cousin hated **classical music**.	My cousin hated **sleeping on the sofa**.
Did Mom mention **Bill's promotion**?	Did Mom mention **meeting the mayor**?
June loved **the art museum**.	June loved **baking**.

It is possible to use a gerund as an indirect object, but that kind of structure can sound awkward and occurs only rarely. For example:

You have strong legs. You should give **running** another chance.

Placement of *not*

You have to use some caution when negating a sentence that contains a gerund serving as a direct object, because the meaning of the sentence is altered by the placement of the adverb **not**. If you negate the verb, the action of the sentence is negated. If you negate the gerund, you are suggesting an alternative to the meaning of the gerund. When you negate a gerund, the adverb **not** should be placed directly in front of the gerund: **not singing**, **not following**, and so on. Let's look at specific examples showing the difference of meaning that occurs by the placement of **not**:

Positive	I'm considering **driving** to Denver.	
Negated verb	I'm **not** considering **driving** to Denver.	*I have no plan to go to Denver.*
Negated object	I'm considering **not driving** to Denver.	*Instead, I'm thinking of flying there.*
Positive	John likes **talking** on the phone.	
Negated verb	John doesn**'t** like **talking** on the phone.	*He prefers talking face-to-face.*
Negated object	John likes **not talking** on the phone.	*He's enjoying avoiding his former habit of talking on the phone.*
Positive	She preferred **wearing** business attire.	
Negated verb	She did**n't** prefer **wearing** business attire.	*Someone misunderstood what she preferred to wear.*
Negated object	She preferred **not wearing** business attire.	*Her preference was casual attire.*

*Using the phrases provided, first write a positive sentence with the gerund serving as a subject, a direct object, or the object of a preposition. Then rewrite the sentence with the gerund negated by **not**.*

EXAMPLE: watching the game

Jim mentioned watching the game today.

Jim mentioned not watching the game today.

1. washing the car

    a. _____

    b. _____

2. vacationing in Florida

    a. _____

    b. _____

3. visiting Uncle Charlie

    a. _____

    b. _____

4. getting up at dawn

    a. _____

    b. _____

5. spending the weekend at the cabin

    a. _____

    b. _____

6. having a wholesome breakfast

    a. _____

    b. _____

Gerunds versus present participles

When gerunds are used as modifiers, remember that they are *nouns used as modifiers*. There is a difference between a gerund and how it modifies, on the one hand, and a present participle and how it modifies. Here's how it breaks down:

◆ Present participle

The man **planning the party** is my uncle.	*the man who is planning = present participle*
The **scratching** dog has fleas.	*the dog that is scratching = present participle*
The **baking** cakes smell delicious.	*the cakes that are baking = present participle*

◆ Gerund

The **planning** department met at four.	*the department that does the planning (noun) = gerund*

That **scratching** noise is very annoying.   *the noise sounds like scratching (noun) =*
                                                      gerund

This is a **baking** dish.   *a dish for baking (noun) = gerund*

*Add the suffix **-ing** to the verb provided, and write any appropriate sentence using that word as a present participle. Then write another appropriate sentence using that word as a gerund.*

EXAMPLE: to take

We are taking a vacation to Montana.

Taking final exams is stressful.

1. to hike

   a. _____

   b. _____

2. to require

   a. _____

   b. _____

3. to suggest

   a. _____

   b. _____

4. to employ

   a. _____

   b. _____

5. to imitate

   a. _____

   b. _____

Follow the same directions, but now write sentences that use the present participle and the gerund as modifiers.

6. to investigate

   a. _____

   b. _____

7. to train

   a. _____

   b. _____

Possessive constructions

Most singular English nouns form their possessive by adding an apostrophe plus *s* to the end of the word; for example, **Jim's, the girl's**. If the noun is plural, those positions are generally switched: the apostrophe follows the *s*; for example, **the boys', the parents'**. In addition, the possessive can often be formed with the preposition **of**; for example, **of the boy, of the university**.

When a gerund is used in the possessive, it is possible to add an apostrophe plus *s*, but it is far more common to make the gerund the object of the preposition **of**. For example:

Possible	More likely
the **burning's** effect	the effect **of the burning**
the **drowning's** cause	the cause **of the drowning**

Since gerunds tend to describe something inanimate, the greater tendency is to use the preposition **of**.

Prepositions with gerunds

A long list of prepositions can be used with gerunds. Some of these prepositions are often paired with specific verbs. For instance, the correct usage is **to be interested "in"** and not **to** or **from** or any other preposition.

Some verbs and adjectives are used primarily with the preposition **for**:

grateful for	to vouch for	responsible for

Some are used with the preposition **of**:

capable of	guilty of	scared of

Some are used with the preposition **to**:

to commit to	to connect to	to dedicate to

Some are used with the preposition **with**:

to bore with	to finish with	to satisfy with

These are just a few examples of the large number of verbs that are accompanied by specific prepositions. Many of them can be used to form a prepositional phrase with a gerund. For example:

to be satisfied with the training	**to be interested in** sailing
to be tired of waiting	**to think about** studying
exhausted from working	**sick of** struggling

When a gerund is placed in the position of an appositive, it functions like any other appositive: it gives further meaning about or describes its antecedent. A gerund acting as an appositive always stands directly after its antecedent. Unlike the case with infinitives, gerunds cannot be used as delayed appositives. For example:

The next step, **planning for the new school year**, will be headed by Jean.
His problem, **worrying about money**, can be solved by a better job.
Jane's reaction, **laughing at my suggestion**, was a real insult.

Using the phrase provided, write an original sentence with the gerund serving as the object of a preposition. Then write a second sentence with the gerund used as an appositive.

EXAMPLE: about the damming of the river

The editorial was about the damming of the river.

This project, the damming of the river, has many dangers.

1. of being your assistant

   a. _____

   b. _____

2. from stopping too suddenly

   a. _____

   b. _____

3. to sunbathing and swimming

   a. _____

   b. _____

4. in razing the old church

   a. _____

   b. _____

5. by playing with matches

   a. _____

   b. _____

Infinitives and gerunds

Infinitives can be used as nouns, and gerunds are always used as nouns. In many cases, therefore, it is possible for infinitives (used as nouns) and gerunds to replace one another in sentences, with little or no change in the meaning of the sentence.

subject + verb + infinitive
subject + verb + gerund

Let's look at some example sentences:

I love **to swim** in a cool lake.	I love **swimming** in a cool lake.
She prefers **to use** her own money.	She prefers **using** her own money.
Did you start **to lose** weight?	Did you start **losing** weight?

This mutual replacement of infinitives and gerunds does not occur with all verbs. Some of the commonly used verbs that can be followed by either an infinitive or a gerund are **to begin**, **to cease**, **to continue**, **to dread**, **to hate**, **to like**, **to love**, **to neglect**, and **to propose**.

Some verbs can be followed only by infinitives. For example:

Did you **decide to buy** the car?   Buying *cannot be used.*
She **wants to help** your family.   Helping *cannot be used.*

See Chapter 12 regarding verbs that require infinitive usage.

There are other verbs that can be followed by either an infinitive or a gerund, but these combinations *sometimes* carry different meanings. Verbs of this type include **to attempt**, **to forget**, **to hope**, **to mean**, **to regret**, **to remember**, and **to try**. Let's look at some of these verbs in sentences and how their meanings vary depending on whether the infinitive or the gerund is used:

Bill **forgot to park** in the garage.   *Bill parked his car somewhere else.*
Bill **forgot parking** in the garage.   *Bill parked in the garage, but he forgot that*
     he did.

I **remember to buy** groceries.   *I don't forget to buy groceries.*
I **remember buying** groceries.   *I'm confused, but there is a memory of*
     buying groceries.

Try to raise your hand.   *See if you can move your injured hand.*
Try raising your hand.   *The teacher will call on you if you raise*
     your hand.

Exercise

13·5

Complete the following sentences twice: first with an infinitive, and then with a gerund wherever possible. If a gerund cannot be used, enter "NA" (i.e., not applicable). Be aware that there may be a difference in meaning between the infinitive and the gerund.

EXAMPLE: We need to start <u>to raise money</u> / <u>raising money</u>.

1. I would love _____ .

2. She always remembers _____ .

3. We need to begin _____ .

4. Tim sometimes hated _____ .

5. Did you always like _____ ?

6. Don't forget _____ .

7. You should try _____ .

8. The judge neglected _____ .

9. You must immediately cease _____ .

10. The little boy continued _____ .

◆14◆ Idioms

Idioms are phrases or sentences that cannot be translated literally from one language to another. They usually comprise common words used in an unexpected way, and that often results in confusion when the student of English is not aware that the words are used idiomatically.

ordinary words + unexpected usage → idiom

Consider the following examples and *what the sentences mean—not what the individual words mean*:

Keep an eye on that for me.	*Watch that for me.*
You're pulling my leg!	*You're joking with me!*
You can bet your bottom dollar that he's right.	*You can be absolutely sure that he's right.*

The appropriate use of idioms and other expressions that carry an unexpected meaning can be an asset in writing good sentences. Although they require care in how they're employed, they can make sentences more interesting by providing a casual tone to a text and even a little fun.

Parts of speech used in idioms

It is not just a single part of speech that can be used idiomatically. Various parts of speech occur in idioms. This section outlines some commonly used idioms based on the part of speech they feature.

Nouns

Many nouns are used idiomatically, and when they are, either their meaning or their function in a sentence is changed. For example:

beeline	She **made a beeline for** the library.	*She went directly to the library.*

Both the subject and the object of the preposition in this idiom can change: **Tom made a beeline for the exit.**

bone	I have **a bone to pick with** you.	*I need to discuss a problem with you.*

Again, both the subject, the object of the preposition, and the tense of the verb in this idiom can change: **She has a bone to pick with her boyfriend.**

126

card	Tom is **a real card**.	*Tom is very funny.*

Only the subject of this idiom can change. The subjects tend to refer to males: **Her husband is a real card.**

dog	His business soon **went to the dogs**.	*His business soon was ruined.*

Only the subject of this idiom can change.

tongue	The answer is **on the tip of my tongue**.	*I can almost remember the answer.*

The subject of the sentence, the possessive, and the tense can change in this idiom: **The man's name was on the tip of her tongue.**

water	You're **in hot water** now!	*You're in a lot of trouble now!*

Only the subject of this idiom can change.

Verbs

Let's turn to some verbs that are used idiomatically:

eat	He had **to eat his (own) words**.	*He was wrong and had to admit to it.*

Only the subject and accompanying possessive of this idiom can change.

feel	Do you **feel like** going out for pizza?	*Do you have a desire to go out for pizza?*

The subject of this idiom can change. The phrase **feel like** should be followed by a gerund: **Did they feel like coming to my party?**

keep	You have **to keep a stiff upper lip**.	*You have to be brave.*

Only the subject of this idiom can change.

paint	The winning team **painted the town red**.	*The winning team had an evening of fun (and drinking).*

Only the subject of this idiom can change.

Adjectives

Here are some adjectives that are used idiomatically:

better	You (**had**) **better** be home on time.	*A warning: Be home on time.*

The subject of the sentence and the verb phrase that follows (**had**) **better** can change: **We better stay home tonight.**

fishy	Your story sounds **fishy (to me)**.	*Your story sounds false (to me).*

The subject and the optional prepositional phrase can be changed in this idiom: **His explanation sounded fishy to the judge.**

hot	That's **a lot of hot air**!	*That sounds like a lie or an exaggeration!*

Only the subject of this idiom can change: **His story is a lot of hot air!**

| red | These forms are just (**a lot of**) **red tape**. | *These forms are just a lot of complicated (governmental) procedures.* |

This idiom can be used after the phrase **a lot of** or as a predicate nominative.

| well | Our neighbors are quite **well off**. | *Our neighbors are quite wealthy.* |

This idiom can be used attributively but is most frequently used predicatively: **Is John really so well off?**

It is common to omit the word **had** from the expression **had better**. For example:

We **had better** check the time of our flight.
We **better** check the time of our flight.

Prepositions

Next, let's look at some prepositions that are used idiomatically:

| about | I **was about to** call him, when he arrived. | *I was ready to call him, when he arrived.* |

This meaning of **about** is preceded by a form of **to be** and followed by infinitive phrases: **Jane was about to get into bed, when the phone rang.**

| from | You'd better start counting **from scratch**. | *You'd better start counting from the beginning.* |

This idiom can be used in most sentences as a replacement for **from the beginning**.

| in | Mary said her sister is **in the family way**. | *Mary said her sister is pregnant.* |

Only the subject of this idiom can change.

| on | My brother is always **on the go**. | *My brother is always in a hurry (or busy).* |

Only the subject of this idiom can change.

| under | I heard him say something **under his breath**. | *I heard him say something in a whisper.* |

This idiom always tells *how* something is said.

Exercise
14·1

Change the underlined word or phrase in each sentence that follows to the corresponding idiom previously illustrated.

EXAMPLE: Jane didn't know she was <u>pregnant</u>.

<u>in the family way</u>

1. My cousin is always <u>joking with me</u>.

_____

2. We were <u>ready</u> to leave, when our neighbor dropped by.

_____

3. I always thought the Johnsons were so <u>wealthy</u>.

_____

4. I really don't <u>have a desire to go</u> out tonight.

_____

5. His reason for his behavior is just <u>an exaggeration</u>.

_____

6. <u>You can be absolutely sure</u> that this stock will go up next week.

_____

7. <u>Don't</u> stay out late.

_____

8. I'm going to check the list again <u>from the beginning</u>.

_____

9. I'm sick of all <u>these governmental procedures</u>!

_____

10. One of my nephews is <u>really funny</u>.

_____

Write two appropriate completions to each of the following sentences containing idioms.

EXAMPLE: _____ in the family way.

Mary knew she was in the family way.

Bill asked his wife whether she is in the family way.

1. _____ under her breath.

   a. _____

   b. _____

2. You never feel like _____.

   a. _____

   b. _____

3. I had better not _____.

   a. _____

   b. _____

4. _____ is on the tip of my tongue.

   a. _____

   b. _____

5. The young woman was about _____.

   a. _____

   b. _____

6. _____ red tape.

   a. _____

   b. _____

7. _____ to eat his (her/my) own words.

   a. _____

   b. _____

Write an original sentence with each of the idiomatic phrases provided.

1. well off

_____

2. hot air

_____

3. from scratch

_____

4. fishy

_____

5. a bone to pick

_____

6. keep a stiff upper lip

_____

7. feel like

_____

8. in hot water

_____

9. (had) better

_____

10. go to the dogs

_____

Special words and phrases

Nearly every language features "little words" or "short phrases" that are added to sentences for emphasis or to give a particular quality to a phrase. Look at the following two sentences. The only difference between the two is the final prepositional phrase in the second sentence:

> I don't care.
> I don't care **in the least**.

The addition of the phrase **in the least** changes the tone of the sentence from casual to emphatic and with a hint of anger. This same prepositional phrase modifies other sentences in a similar way. For example:

I'm not interested in that.	I'm not interested in that **in the least**.
I don't believe you.	I don't believe you **in the least**.
I'm not aware of that.	I'm not **in the least** aware of that.

This section highlights other words and phrases that modify the meanings of sentences.

At all

The two little words **at all** when added to a negative sentence emphasize the degree of negativity. It is the adverb **not** that is modified by this phrase. With linking verbs, the phrase **at all** follows the adverb **not** or another negative word, or it can be placed after the predicate nominative. Let's look at some examples:

I'm not **at all pleased** by this.	I'm not **pleased at all** by this.
Sarah wasn't **at all impressed**.	Sarah wasn't **impressed at all**.
He isn't **at all rich**.	He isn't **rich at all**.

With other verbs, **at all** tends to be placed after the verb or verb phrase. For example:

Bill wouldn't speak **with her at all**.
I actually have no opinion **about it at all**.
He didn't ask **about her condition at all**.

By the way

The phrase **by the way** is usually added at the beginning of a sentence, although it sometimes can occur in a medial or final position. It indicates that the speaker or writer *doesn't want to forget to mention something*. Let's look at some sentences that illustrate this usage:

Bill's team won the trophy. **By the way**, I'm on that team, too.
By the way, I ran into your brother last night.
I'll be at your party. **By the way**, do you mind if I bring along Tina?

How about

How about is used to introduce a question that asks whether someone is *interested in doing something*. Consider this question: **Are you interested in going to the movies?** It can be restated like this: **How about going to the movies?** Let's look at a couple more examples:

How about spending some time with Uncle Fred?
How about trying to save a little more money?

Mind

This verb usually means *to see after* or *to tend to*. It can also be used to mean *to pay strict attention to* or *to be on guard against*. Yet another useful application is its meaning of *to care about* or *to have anything against* an idea or action. It is also used to say that someone *has the urge* or *wants to do something*. For example:

Do you mind if I sit here?	*Do you care that I sit here?/Do you have anything against my sitting here?*
No, **I don't mind**.	*No, I don't care./No, I have nothing against your sitting here.*
I wouldn't mind having a nice cold beer right now.	*I have the urge to have a cold beer right now.*

Or so

The phrase **or so** is a synonym for *approximately* or *about*. Compare the following pairs of sentences:

She's approximately thirty years old.	She's thirty years old **or so**.
The turkey weighed about twenty pounds.	The turkey weighed twenty pounds **or so**.

Notice that **or so** is positioned after the quantity it modifies.

Really

The word **really** can be used in a variety of sentence types. It can serve as an adverb that means *as a matter of fact* or *in reality*. It is also commonly used to *emphasize* certain elements in a sentence, primarily verbs, adjectives, and other adverbs.

- ◆ Modifying verbs

I don't like that man.	I **really** don't like that man.
Do you want to buy that old car?	Do you **really** want to buy that old car?
The men had a lot of fun at the ball game.	The men **really** had a lot of fun at the ball game.

- ◆ Modifying adjectives

Sarah bought an expensive dress.	Sarah bought a **really** expensive dress.
That's a good copy of the map.	That's a **really** good copy of the map.
John bought some cheap wine.	John bought some **really** cheap wine.

- ◆ Modifying other adverbs

Granddad drove carefully.	Granddad drove **really** carefully.
Did they get up early?	Did they get up **really** early?
I never understood his motives.	I **really** never understood his motives.

Should have

The valuable little phrase **should have** implies that something that occurred was *regrettable*. In the negative, it suggests that something that occurred was a *mistake*. The subject of this verb phrase can be most any noun or pronoun:

- ◆ Positive

You **should have called** me yesterday.	*It's regrettable that you didn't call.*
Should I **have told** her about my illness?	*Should I regret that I didn't tell her?*
Tom **should have married** Marie.	*It's regrettable that he didn't marry her.*

- ◆ Negative

I **shouldn't have spoken** to him that way.	*It was a mistake to speak to him that way.*
They **shouldn't have left** today.	*It was a mistake for them to leave today.*
Jane **shouldn't have gone out** with Joe.	*It was a mistake for her to go out with Joe.*

Well

The word **well** has more than one function in English. It is the adverb for the adjective **good**, and it is the adjective that means *healthy* and is the opposite of *sick*. It is also used as an interjection, but because it has idiomatic qualities, it needs to be looked at again.

Well can be used to *stall for a little time*, often in response to a difficult or uncomfortable comment. For example:

> —I expect you in my office in an hour.
> —**Well**, let me check my calendar.

> —Can you answer my question?
> —**Well**, let me think about that for a moment.

It also introduces a sentence that expresses *surprise*. Although *surprise* can be expressed without the interjection, the addition of **well** provides emphasis.

> **Well**, I had no idea that you'd be here today.
> **Well**, I certainly didn't expect to get a speeding ticket.

In can also express *impatience*. Compare the following pairs of sentences:

No interjection	Interjection indicating impatience
Are you ready?	**Well**, are you ready?
You're going to be late again.	**Well**, you're going to be late again.

Exercise 14·4

*Fill in the blank in each sentence with the word or phrase from the following list that makes the most sense: **at all, by the way, how about, mind, or so, really,** or **should have.***

EXAMPLE: She chose a <u>really</u> expensive ring.

1. I'm not happy _____ with the outcome.

2. Do you _____ understand this poem?

3. We _____ asked Aunt Louise for some financial help.

4. Did her brother _____ that you asked her out?

5. _____ , it's hard for me to explain.

6. John joined the marines, and, _____ , so did I.

7. I think the center of the team is seven feet tall _____ .

8. _____ going out for some dinner with me?

9. Professor Smith is a _____ refined gentleman.

10. It's none of your business _____ .

Exercise 14·5

Write two original sentences containing each of the words or phrases provided.

1. really

   a. _____

   b. _____

2. mind

   a. _____

   b. _____

3. at all

   a. _____

   b. _____

4. should have

   a. _____

   b. _____

5. or so

   a. _____

   b. _____

6. go to the dogs

   a. _____

   b. _____

7. by the way

   a. _____

   b. _____

8. how about

   a. _____

   b. _____

9. well

   a. _____

   b. _____

10. feel like

    a. _____

    b. _____

Short responses and interjections

·15·

Not all powerful sentences are long. Even short sentences can carry a lot of meaning, especially when they are the response to a question or statement whose meaning is understood in the reply. For instance, the individual words **fine** and **hardly** have their own meanings, but they can also stand alone as an elliptical response to a question or statement.

—You'll have to stay home tonight and study.
—**Fine.**   *Fine, I accept the fact that I must stay home and study.*

—I suppose you're going to vote for Laura as chairperson.
—**Hardly.**   *Your supposition is hardly correct. I'll vote for Marie.*

Short responses

Many individual words and brief phrases can be used as short responses to questions or statements. Consider the following list:

Amazing!	Of course.
Apparently.	Outstanding!
Don't mention it.	Really?
Excellent!	Terrific!
For heaven's sake!	That depends.
Fortunately.	That's great.
I have no idea.	That's hard to believe.
Impossible.	Unbelievable!
Incredible.	Unfortunately, no/not.
It can't be (true)!	What a pity.
Naturally.	What do you mean?
Not at all.	You're kidding/not serious.
Obviously.	You're welcome.

Naturally, words and phrases such as these do not have a singular use. They can respond to numerous questions or statements; likewise, there can be numerous short responses to a single question or statement. Here are examples:

◆ Various statements/same response

—John is a wonderful tennis player.
—**Really?**

—I simply can't afford a vacation now.
—**Really?**

—Does Tim have a new job?
—**I have no idea.**

—Is Mark remarried?
—**I have no idea.**

136

♦ Same statement/various responses

—Is your sister back from college? —Is your sister back from college?
—**Unfortunately, not.** —**Of course.**

—Mr. Garcia won the lottery! —Mr. Garcia won the lottery!
—**Terrific!** —**You're kidding!**

EXERCISE
15·1

Respond to the following questions and statements with one of the words or phrases listed in the preceding section.

EXAMPLE: Thanks for helping out with the party.

You're welcome.

1. Do you have to work this Saturday?

_____

2. I really appreciate your support. Thanks.

_____

3. The dog knocked over Mom's new vase.

_____

4. Is winter going to last much longer?

_____

5. Will the new girl be joining us for dinner?

_____

6. My cousin lost his job and can't afford his apartment.

_____

7. Our school's soccer team won first place!

_____

8. Are you interested in working abroad?

_____

9. It seems that the other candidate will win the election.

_____

10. Did the operation go well?

_____

Write an appropriate question or statement for each of the responses provided.

EXAMPLE: <u>Despite some bad grades, you're going to graduate.</u> Excellent!

1. _____ Incredible.

2. _____ That depends.

3. _____ Amazing!

4. _____ What a pity.

5. _____ Apparently.

6. _____ Not at all.

7. _____ What do you mean?

8. _____ Unfortunately, no.

9. _____ Outstanding!

10. _____ For heaven's sake.

Interjections

Interjections are words that are used to express strong emotion. They can appear alone or as part of a sentence. They give a text a casual tone and, therefore, are rarely used in formal writing. Here is a roster of some common interjections:

ah	great	now	there
aha	here	O	well
alas	hurrah	oh	what
bravo	indeed	ouch	why
good	my	see	wow
goodness	no	so	yes

Besides showing emotion as an exclamation, an interjection can also function as a parenthetical word. Its position is most often at the beginning of a sentence or clause, but interjections can sometimes occur elsewhere in a sentence. If an interjection is written by itself, it is most often punctuated with an exclamation point. The examples that follow illustrate how sentences change when an interjection is added to them:

Stand near the piano.	*a casual command*
No! Stand near the piano.	*an abrupt correction to someone standing in the wrong place*
That wound looks serious.	*a casual statement*
Ouch! That wound looks serious.	*an expression of sympathy for the injured person*
The cold water tastes good.	*a casual statement*
Ah, the cold water tastes good.	*an expression of satisfaction that the person's thirst is being quenched*

Most of the interjections listed in this section are self-explanatory. However, some require a little clarification.

We'll start with the difference between **ah** and **aha** and proceed alphabetically. The use of **ah** shows delight or comfort, while the use of **aha** announces that a truth has been discovered or a secret revealed.

> **Ah!** You spelled that word just right.
> **Ah**, that feels good.

> **Aha!** You're the thief!
> **Aha!** I see you've hidden the map behind this portrait.

Although the word **alas** sounds somewhat archaic, it is still used in many forms of writing to provide a *lofty tone* and to express regret or disappointment. It is usually interchangeable with **unfortunately**.

> **Alas**, despite hours of negotiations, the treaty was not signed.
> Their efforts to secure a peace were, **alas**, a failure.

The normal meaning and use of **goodness** (decency, honesty, kindness) is lost when that word is used as an interjection. It gives the idea that the speaker or writer is somewhat shocked:

> **Goodness**, that was a close call.
> **Goodness!** Why are you dressed like that?

The possessive **my** can be used as an interjection, but when it is, it no longer has to do with possession. Rather, it expresses the idea of mild shock or mild delight. For example:

> **My**, that was a harsh thing to say to him.
> **My**, I really like the way you look in that dress.

The adverb **now** does not describe time when it functions as an interjection. Instead, it means that a suggestion is about to be stated.

> **Now**, start again and play that melody with greater emotion.
> **Now**, let's not argue about that again.

There is a difference between **O** and **oh**. The use of **O** is *vocative*; it addresses a person or persons and suggests passion or is used in prayer. The interjection **oh** is used to express sudden emotion or surprise. Many writers use it in place of **O**.

> **O** Lord! Hear my prayer!
> **O**, all men of goodwill, join me in this crusade.

> **Oh**, I love the evening view over the Grand Canyon.
> **Oh**, I didn't see you standing there.

The verb **see** has nothing to do with vision when it serves as an interjection. It implies that someone needs to be aware of a situation or that someone has failed to heed a warning.

> **See**, this is how you hem a skirt properly.
> **See!** I told you that you'd ruin that old clock if you wound it too tightly.

When **there** is used as an interjection, its meaning does not indicate a place. Instead, it points out how something is done or suggests that an unwanted situation has developed.

> **There**, that's the way to slice a turkey breast.
> **There!** You had to go on that hike, and now you have a bad cold!

The word **what** is used with two different kinds of interjections. One is a question that carries the interrogative meaning of **what** but with strong emotion. The other does not ask a question but instead exclaims marked disbelief. For example:

> **What?** Tell me that again! I can't believe my ears!
> **What!** It's a lie! The man is a liar!

The interrogative **why** is no interrogative at all when it is used as an interjection. It says, instead, that something is unbelievable or a contradiction.

> **Why**, there's no such thing as an elf!
> **Why**, you can't really believe that story.

Exercise 15·3

In the space provided, enter an appropriate interjection for the intent of each sentence.

EXAMPLE: <u>My</u>, having dinner out tonight is a dandy idea.

1. _____ , look what you've done now!

2. _____ , I love the way you give a back massage.

3. _____ , you've found your keys. Now we can finally leave.

4. _____ ! That was an outstanding performance!

5. _____ ! That must have caused you a lot of pain.

6. _____ ! Our team has won the championship again!

7. _____ ! You lied to me, and now you're in a lot of trouble.

8. _____ , you want to be a movie star.

9. _____ , it's getting late. I had better go home.

10. _____ ! Don't touch that wire! You'll get a shock!

Exercise 15·4

Write an original sentence with each of the interjections provided.

1. now _____

2. ah _____

3. great _____

4. see _____

5. there _____

6. well _____

7. why _____

8. here _____

9. so _____

10. indeed _____

Antonyms and contrasts

People often study antonyms as a way of developing vocabulary, but being knowledgeable about antonyms is also an aid in learning to write better sentences. Using pairs of opposites, as well as other words that are not true antonyms but still show a real contrast, can be helpful in developing good sentences.

It is wrong to think that antonyms just describe opposite meanings, such as in the following examples:

> John isn't **tall** but **short**.
> The fish wasn't **dead** but **alive**.
> Mary wanted to be **rich**, but she's **poor**.

Strong contrasts

Illustrating a difference by using contrasting words can help to make a strong point. For instance, instead of just describing someone or something with a single adjective, it is possible to emphasize a quality by employing contrasts. Here is an example:

> The villain in the story cannot be described as a **good** man, for his lying, cheating, and attempts at deception proved him to be the worst among the **bad**.

You likely are familiar with a variety of antonyms and contrasts. Many are basic to the study of language. Some commonly used pairs of contrasting words are listed here:

all/none	day/night	often/seldom
always/never	dirty/clean	right/wrong
beautiful/ugly	early/late	send/receive
before/after	easy/difficult	smart/stupid
below/above	empty/full	start/finish
black/white	find/lose	wet/dry
dark/light	hot/cold	young/old

Using the following pairs of words, write sentences that make a simple contrast.

EXAMPLE: long/short

He needed a long rope but found only a short one.

1. easy/difficult

_____

2. empty/full

_____

3. find/lose

_____

4. often/seldom

_____

5. right/wrong

_____

6. send/receive

_____

7. smart/stupid

_____

8. start/finish

_____

9. wet/dry

_____

10. young/old

_____

There are numerous pairs of contrasting words, and most of them can be employed to make a special point in a sentence—*a contrast for emphasis*. Although the meanings of the individual words may be simple, the effect can be impressive when they're used in this way. For instance, if you use a simple pair of words such as **give/take** in this manner, you can come up with interesting sentences that go beyond *a simple contrast*. Here are two examples:

> Their neighbor was not known for **giving**, not of himself nor or his earthly goods; he was infamous, however, for his **taking**: **taking** what didn't belong to him, **taking** away a person's valuable time, and **taking** the joy out of life.

> I **gave** her all my love, and she **took** it gladly along with my self-respect and every penny I had saved.

Exercise

16·2

Using each pair of words provided, write a sentence that makes an emphatic point as illustrated in the preceding examples.

1. all/none

_____

2. always/never

_____

3. beautiful/ugly

_____

4. before/after

_____

5. below/above

_____

6. black/white

_____

7. dark/light

_____

8. day/night

_____

9. dirty/clean

_____

10. early/late

_____

Some antonyms describe a more complex or abstract contrast and are therefore somewhat more difficult to use. Words such as **absent/present** require that you do a bit more thinking when using them in a sentence.

> The old woman's physical body was **present** at the dinner table, but her thoughts and her soul were **absent** and searching a thousand miles away for the life she had led as a girl.

The following list contains pairs of words that have a more complex or abstract relationship:

abundant/scarce	cruel/kind	imaginary/real
accept/refuse	deep/shallow	increase/decrease
bitter/sweet	discourage/encourage	outer/inner
cheerful/sad	double/single	reward/punishment
combine/separate	drunk/sober	strengthen/weaken
comedy/tragedy	graceful/clumsy	truth//lie
crooked/straight	guilty/innocent	victory/defeat

These pairs of words can be used to make a simple contrast, but because they are more complex or abstract than a pair such as **big/little**, the effect in a sentence can be a loftier tone. Compare the following sentences:

> He wanted to be **big**, but he was only a **little** man.
> He wanted to be **deep**, but he was only a **shallow** man.

Exercise 16·3

Complete each sentence that follows with a phrase that contains the appropriate antonym or contrasting word for the one provided in the first part of the sentence.

EXAMPLE: The pond was shallow near the dock, but in the middle it was dangerously deep.

1. There is no comedy in what you say _____ .

2. A crooked path meandered through the woods _____ .

3. His letter seemed so cruel _____ .

4. I can neither discourage you from this venture _____ .

5. She saw a double figure of a man _____ .

6. The revelers were drunk with joy _____ .

7. For a large man he moved gracefully _____ .

8. She pronounced her husband guilty _____ .

9. Some say that ghosts are imaginary _____ .

10. The victory over the enemy was costly _____ .

Certain other pairs of contrasting words are even more abstract. Their use generally requires employing more complex sentences. Let's look at some examples:

The fall harvest was usually **abundant**, but this year the wheat crop was **scarce**.
He claimed their meeting was **accidental**, but she knew he had shown up **intentionally**.
The regiment struggled to **advance**, but there was only **retreat** in their fate.
I come not to **condemn** this man but to **praise** him.
The nation had been **conquered**, but the spirit of the people knew no **surrender**.
Their failed business was no **disgrace**, but there was likewise no **honor** in it.
Before the drought the fields were **fertile** with crops; now they lay **barren** under the sun.
Where once the people knew **harmony** there now was only **discord**.
In the South they know no **harsh** winters and enjoy a **mild** climate year-round.
I thought my heart was **unbreakable**, but I learned the hard way that it was as **fragile** as crystal.

Complete each sentence that follows with a phrase that contains the appropriate antonym or contrasting word for the one provided in the second part of the sentence.

1. _____ , and they could only hope for an abundant crop next year.

2. _____ , his use of the word *liar* was intentional.

3. _____ , if you retreat in every debate with the boss?

4. _____ , but I also have no praise for her.

5. _____ , but it cannot be conquered.

6. _____ , the former hero died in disgrace.

7. _____ , yet she had become barren in her later years.

8. _____ , they only wished to live in harmony with their neighbors.

9. _____ , but his angry words were harsh.

10. _____ , it is as unbreakable as my will.

Prefixes and suffixes

Some pairs of contrasting words are formed from the use of two common suffixes: **-ful** and **-less**. The suffix **-ful** indicates an abundance of the quality of the adjective to which it is attached. For example:

hateful   *having an abundance of hate, or full of hate*

The suffix **-less** suggests a lack of the quality of the adjective to which it is attached. For example:

childless   *having no children, or barren*

Not all adjectives can be combined with both suffixes. Review the following list of adjectives, some of which use both suffixes and some of which use only one:

-FUL	-LESS
bashful	—
careful	careless
cheerful	cheerless
—	guiltless
grateful	—
helpful	helpless
hopeful	hopeless
—	lifeless
mindful	mindless
restful	restless
—	senseless
—	shapeless
sinful	sinless
—	speechless
spiteful	—
thankful	thankless
—	timeless
useful	useless
—	winless
wonderful	—

Pairing these words can make for interesting sentences. Let's look at a few examples:

John was neither **sinful** nor **sinless** but just an ordinary man.
She was always **mindful** of his physical needs yet **mindless** of his emotions.
I'm **thankful** that you helped me with this **thankless** task.

As noted, some words combine with only one of these two suffixes. Nevertheless, those that combine with both can still be used singly without the need of showing a contrast.

◆ Adjectives with one suffix

Her **lifeless** body lay on the bed where she had died.
Old Mr. Cane was a **spiteful** and bitter man.
How **wonderful** to be back in my homeland.

◆ Adjectives that can take both suffixes

The boys have been **helpful** today.
The elderly man was in a **helpless** state and unable to speak.
This old machinery is hardly **useful** in a big project like this.
It's **useless** for you to try to explain such bad behavior.

Complete each sentence that follows with a phrase that contains the appropriate antonym or contrasting word.

1. Although he was usually careful when handling these chemicals, _____ .

2. _____ , but his mood was cheerless.

3. I was still hopeful _____ .

4. Although I found the room restful, _____ .

5. The tearful woman was truly thankful, _____ .

6. You have to be mindful of the fact that _____ .

7. _____ , Martin tried to be helpful.

8. _____ , no person is sinless.

9. _____ , her attempt to help was useless.

10. Tom made a cheerful noise _____ .

Write original sentences with the adjectives provided.

1. bashful _____

2. guiltless _____

3. grateful _____

4. lifeless _____

5. senseless _____

6. shapeless _____

7. speechless _____

8. spiteful _____

9. timeless _____

10. homeless _____

The prefixes **un-** and **mis-** can be used to change many adjectives and nouns to a negative or contrasting construction. The prefix **un-** is synonymous with *not*, while the prefix **mis-** says that the action of a verb is performed incorrectly. In some cases, the two prefixes can be used with the same word, but with a different meaning being derived.

NO PREFIX	THE PREFIX *UN-*	
able	unable	*not able, or incapable*
broken	unbroken	*not broken after a mishap*
just	unjust	*not just or fair*
likely	unlikely	*not likely, rare*
shaken	unshaken	*not shaken, still calm*

NO PREFIX	THE PREFIX *MIS-*	
calculate	miscalculate	*calculate or analyze incorrectly*
handle	mishandle	*handle poorly, or bungle*
represent	misrepresent	*represent something as something else*
speak	misspeak	*make a spoken error*
treat	mistreat	*treat badly or cruelly*

Numerous words sport these prefixes. You can employ them to give your sentences a more formal tone. Consider the following two sentences; they say about the same thing, but the second example sounds more formal:

John figured it out wrong.   John **miscalculated**.

There are also many words that use both **un-** and **mis-** as prefixes. The meanings of such words must be differentiated. Let's look at some examples:

misinformed	*informed incorrectly*
uninformed	*not informed*
misarranged	*arranged incorrectly*
unarranged	*not arranged*
misnamed	*named incorrectly*
unnamed	*not named*

Other forms of the prefix *un-*

The form of the prefix **un-** can change slightly, depending on the vowel or consonant that follows it, although the meaning of *not* still pertains. For example, **un-** becomes **in-** with some words:

inaccurate	inefficient
inadequate	inexpensive
indivisible	infrequent

Likewise, the prefix changes to **im-** sometimes. This frequently occurs when the prefix is attached to a word that begins with the letter *m*. For example:

immature	immodest
immeasurable	immoral
immobile	immortal

Note also that the prefix **ig-** replaces **un-** with the adjective **ignoble**, which means *not noble*, or *lowborn*. The same prefix is encountered with a few other words, for which there is no contrasting form in English. Examples include the related words **ignore**, **ignorant**, and **ignoramus**.

The prefix *dis-*

Another prefix that imparts a contrasting or negative meaning to some words is **dis-**. Here are some examples:

appear	disappear	*no longer appearing, vanish*
comfort	discomfort	*being uncomfortable*
content	discontent	*lack of contentment, uneasiness*
honest	dishonest	*not honest*

Just as with other prefixes, this one cannot be attached to a word at random. Over time, only certain words have combined with **dis-** to yield a contrasting or negative meaning. Also as with other prefixes, **dis-** can combine with most kinds of words: nouns, verbs, adjectives, and adverbs. Let's look at some sample sentences that illustrate the use of this prefix:

I'm surprised at just how **discourteous** the salesman was.
His **disgraceful** behavior has landed him in a lot of hot water.
Their youngest daughter has become rather **disobedient**.
The surgical instruments need to be **disinfected**.

Exercise 16·7

*Write original sentences containing each of the words provided. Begin each sentence with a clause that starts with **although**.*

EXAMPLE: mistaken Although Larry was usually right, this time he was mistaken.

1. ignoble _____

2. unnatural _____

3. misunderstand _____

4. unsolved _____

5. misbehave _____

Write original sentences using each of the words and phrases provided.

6. discouraged from _____

7. dissatisfy _____

8. severe disability _____

9. displeasing manner _____

10. discontinue _____

The passive voice and the subjunctive mood

The passive voice is so named because it places the subject of an active-voice sentence—the "doer" of the action—in a passive position in the passive-voice sentence. In some cases, it is even possible to omit the doer of the action completely. English has two forms of passive: one contains a past participle used as a verb, and the other contains a past participle used as an adjective.

The passive voice and past participles

The English active voice consists of a subject, a transitive verb, and a direct or indirect object. If those elements occur, the sentence can be changed to a passive-voice sentence. Sentences that contain intransitive verbs cannot be made passive.

> **subject + transitive verb + object**

> John + bought + a new car.

Let's look first at some examples of active-voice sentences:

◆ Sentences with a transitive verb

> Jill **recommended** the movie.
> They **have never met** Mr. Carlson.
> **Did** you **already repair** the garage door?

◆ Sentences with an intransitive verb

> We **went swimming** in Lake Michigan.
> My cousin **was** in Iraq for ten months.
> The girls **came** home around ten P.M.

A passive-voice sentence consists of a subject, a form of **to be**, a past participle, and an optional prepositional phrase introduced by the preposition **by**. When an active sentence is changed to passive, the direct or indirect object of the active sentence becomes the subject of the passive sentence. The verb in the active sentence determines the tense of **to be** in the passive sentence and is formed as a past participle. The active subject is changed to the object of the preposition **by** in the passive sentence.

> **subject + *to be* + past participle**

> The book + had been + stolen.

Let's now look at an active sentence and how it is changed to the passive voice:

| Active | Michael **chased** the little girl across the playground. |
| Passive | The little girl **was chased** across the playground **by** Michael. |

In the active-voice example, the verb is in the past tense—**chased**. Therefore, in the passive sentence, the verb **to be** is conjugated in the past tense—**was**. If the active verb had been **chases**, the verb **is** would have been used. If the active verb had been **will chase**, the verb **will be** would have been used.

Now let's look at active sentences in other tenses and how they are changed to the passive voice:

Active	Someone **is breaking** the window.	*present progressive*
Passive	The window **is being broken**.	*by someone*
Active	They **have built** a moat around the castle.	*present perfect*
Passive	A moat **has been built** around the castle.	*by them*
Active	The angry father **will punish** the naughty boy.	*future*
Passive	The naughty boy **will be punished**.	*by the angry father*

Exercise

17·1

Using each set of words provided, first write an active sentence in the tense specified in parentheses. Then rewrite the sentence in the passive voice.

1. (past) she / learn / several / new / songs

   a. _____

   b. _____

2. (present progressive) bartender / pour / two / beer

   a. _____

   b. _____

3. (present perfect) Andrea / borrow / new / SUV

   a. _____

   b. _____

4. (future) we / never / catch / huge / fish

   a. _____

   b. _____

5. (past progressive) Jack / carefully / photograph / scene / of / accident

   a. _____

   b. _____

6. (present) I / usually / lead / band

   a. _____

   b. _____

7. (past perfect) farmer / plow / field / by late afternoon

a. _____

b. _____

8. (past progressive) pianist / play / sonata / without error

a. _____

b. _____

Why use the passive voice?

The passive voice comes in handy when the writer wishes to emphasize the object of an active sentence: the object becomes the subject of the passive sentence.

The boy **almost hurt** the little puppy.	*direct object*
The little puppy **was almost hurt** by the boy.	*subject*
He **ripped** her dress.	*direct object*
Her dress **was ripped** by him.	*subject*

It is also used when the writer wishes to omit the doer of the action. This choice can reflect the writer's intention to be evasive or to be tactful by not identifying the doer. For example:

The mayor will fire the entire office staff.	
The entire office staff will be fired.	*The writer chooses not to identify the mayor as the responsible party.*
An angry mob beat the poor man bloody.	
The poor man was beaten bloody.	*The writer does not name the guilty party.*

Another use of the passive voice is for sentences in which no specific doer of the action is involved. This often occurs when the subject of the active sentence is vague: **they**, **people**, **some people**, **many**, and **one**, among others.

They grow blueberries in Michigan.
Blueberries **are grown** in Michigan.

People accused Mr. Thomas of being dishonest.
Mr. Thomas **was accused** of being dishonest.

Exercise
17·2

*Rewrite the following active-voice sentences in the passive voice. Do not include a **by** phrase in your passive sentences.*

1. They grow oranges and lemons in this region of California.

_____

2. Some people have already identified the thief.

_____

3. He is painting her portrait as a surprise for her husband.

   _____

4. People will greet him enthusiastically.

   _____

5. They repaired and repainted the old car.

   _____

6. Despite the inconsistencies, many believed his story.

   _____

7. Some have recommended Ms. Lopez for the job.

   _____

8. They were examining the evidence in preparation for the trial.

   _____

9. Someone has noted his strange behavior in the final report.

   _____

10. Did anyone recognize him?

   _____

If a writer wishes to conceal his or her source of information, the impersonal **it** can be used as the subject of a passive phrase that serves to introduce another clause. For example:

> It **has been reported** that the country is in a recession.
> It **is widely believed** that humans evolved from apes.

Exercise 17·3

*Using the verbs provided, write original passive sentences with the impersonal **it** as the subject. Provide an appropriate accompanying clause for each.*

EXAMPLE: believe It is believed that nearly a hundred people were injured in the accident.

1. report _____

2. state _____

3. remark _____

4. prove _____

5. write _____

6. announce _____

7. estimate _____

8. decide _____

9. mention _____

10. argue _____

Direct and indirect objects

If the active sentence contains both a direct object and an indirect object, the passive formations of that sentence differ and depend on which object is made the subject of the passive sentence. For example:

James gave the **poor man five dollars**.　　　the poor man = *indirect object*;
　　　　　　　　　　　　　　　　　　　　　　　five dollars = *direct object*

The poor man was given five dollars by James.　*indirect object as subject*
Five dollars was given to the poor man by James.　*direct object as subject*

If the direct object is the subject of the passive sentence, the indirect object requires the use of the preposition **to**.

Five dollars was given **to** the poor man by James.

Rewrite the following active sentences in the passive voice twice: first with the direct object used as the passive subject, and then with the indirect object used as the passive subject.

1. The woman sent him a counterfeit check.

　a. _____

　b. _____

2. I will lend the man a shirt and tie.

　a. _____

　b. _____

3. Aunt Mary is shipping us a crate of oranges.

　a. _____

　b. _____

4. Were the judges awarding them a medal?

　a. _____

　b. _____

5. The broker has shown the young couple two new houses.

　a. _____

　b. _____

Auxiliaries and the passive

As the passive voice is expressed in the various tenses, the verb **to be** has to be conjugated appropriately. In the perfect tenses, the auxiliary **have** is the conjugated verb, and **to be** is formed as the past participle **been**.

> **has/have/had + been + past participle**

> I have + been + robbed.

Let's look at the passive voice in the various tenses:

Present	She **is kissed** by Ben. / She **is being kissed** by Ben.
Past	She **was kissed** by Ben. / She **was being kissed** by Ben.
Present perfect	She **has been kissed** by Ben.
Past perfect	She **had been kissed** by Ben.
Future	She **will be kissed** by Ben.

Other auxiliaries often accompany the passive voice as well. When this is the case, it is the auxiliary that is conjugated in a specific tense, and the passive-voice structure is a passive infinitive. The passive infinitive is always **to be** plus a past participle.

> **auxiliary + *to be* + past participle**

> It must + be + repaired today.

Some commonly used auxiliaries are **can**, **have to**, **must**, **want to**, **ought to**, **should**, and **be able to**. Let's look at a few sample sentences with some of these auxiliaries in various tenses:

Your suit **can** be cleaned and pressed by four P.M.	*present tense*
The meeting **will have to** be postponed.	*future tense*
Didn't you **want to** be chosen for the job?	*past tense*
Jake **will** be added to the team by Coach Brown.	*future auxiliary*

Not all auxiliaries can be used in all the tenses. **Can**, **must**, **ought to**, and **should**, for example, occur only in the present and past tenses. Their past-tense forms are, respectively, **could**, **must have**, **ought to have**, and **should have**. The auxiliaries **have to**, **be able to**, and **want to** occur in all the tenses. Let's look at one of these auxiliaries—**want to**—in the various tenses:

Present	Laura **wants to be taken** more seriously.
Past	Laura **wanted to be taken** more seriously.
Present perfect	Laura **has wanted to be taken** more seriously.
Past perfect	Laura **had wanted to be taken** more seriously.
Future	Laura **will want to be taken** more seriously.

It is only the auxiliary that changes in the various tenses. The passive-voice form remains a passive infinitive (**to be taken**) throughout.

When **must have**, **ought to have**, and **should have** are followed by the passive voice, the passive structure consists of **been** plus a past participle.

> She **must have been warned** about his temper.
> We **ought to have been paid** a little more money.
> You **should have been rewarded** for such a good deed.

Rewrite the following passive sentences using the auxiliaries provided in parentheses; retain the tense of the original sentence.

EXAMPLE: (can) She was seen by a group of people.

<u>She could be seen by a group of people.</u>

1. (must) Robert is rushed to the hospital.

_____

2. (have to) Someone is held responsible for any act of vandalism.

_____

3. (should) I was not found guilty.

_____

4. (want to) These men will be paid fairly.

_____

5. (can) The other teams aren't instructed by professionals.

_____

6. (must) The roof was struck by lightning.

_____

7. (be able to) No one was rescued.

_____

8. (want to) This student had been admitted to the university.

_____

9. (ought to) The diplomats are greeted by the head of state.

_____

10. (have to) Grandfather has been operated on.

_____

The stative passive

As mentioned earlier, there is a second type of passive. It consists of a conjugation of the verb **to be** plus a past participle. That, of course, sounds like the previous description of the passive voice. The difference is not so much in the structure as it is in the meaning and usage of the past participle. This second passive, called the *stative passive*, uses the past participle as an adjective. Consider the following two sentences in the present tense:

The old clock **is being repaired**.
The old clock **is repaired**.

The first sentence conveys an action that is in progress, and the participle **repaired** is in the passive voice. The second sentence describes the clock as already being *in a state of repair*. It is adjectival in nature and, therefore, in the stative passive voice.

When the progressive form of the verb is used (**is being repaired**), the past participle describes the action of a verb; the structure is, therefore, not the stative passive. A prepositional phrase introduced by the preposition **by** is another indicator that the past participle is not adjectival.

The dish is broken.	*stative passive*
The dish is broken by Jack.	*action in the passive voice*
The bread is sliced.	*stative passive*
The bread is sliced by a special machine.	*action in the passive voice*

The stative passive tends to occur in the present tense. However, if the intent of the writer is to apply the past participle as an adjective, other tenses can be used. In such constructions, the adjectival meaning may not always be clear. Consider the following past participles used in the stative passive:

Present	This cup is broken.	*Its condition is "broken." It requires repair.*
Past	This cup was broken.	*It used to be broken. It has been glued together.*
Present perfect	This cup has been broken for more than a month.	*It's been in a broken condition for more than a month.*
Past perfect	This cup had been broken but is now whole again.	*It used to be broken. It has been glued together.*
Future	This cup will be broken.	*The prediction is that its condition in the future will be "broken."*

If you replace the word **broken** with a true adjective, such as **yellow**, the adjectival function of the past participle becomes clear. If **yellow** can replace a past participle and make sense, then the past participle is being used as an adjective. If it makes no sense, the past participle is a verb in the passive voice. Compare the following sentences:

This cup is broken.	This cup is yellow.	
This cup is broken by Tom.	This cup is yellow by Tom.	*Makes no sense.*
The clock was repaired.	The clock was yellow.	
The clock was repaired by her.	The clock was yellow by her.	*Makes no sense.*
She is being punished.	She is being yellow.	*Makes no sense.*
She is being punished by Mom.	She is being yellow by Mom.	*Makes no sense.*

When the verb **to be** is conjugated in the progressive present tense or progressive past tense, it is clear that the past participle is part of the passive-voice structure. When the progressive conjugation is not used, though, that clarity of meaning is lost, and the sentence could be interpreted as either the passive voice or the stative passive. The addition of a **by** phrase makes the passive voice meaning clear.

Passive voice/progressive tense	**Passive voice or stative passive**
The dog **is being** washed.	The dog **is** washed.
The field **was being** cleared.	The field **was** cleared.

Passive voice/progressive tense + by

The dog **is being** washed **by** John.
The field **was being** cleared **by** the men.

Passive voice + by

The dog **is** washed **by** John.
The field **was** cleared **by** the men.

Whether a past participle is being used as part of a passive-voice structure or as an adjective is wholly *dependent on the writer's intent*, and the reader cannot always guess correctly what the writer has intended. Therefore, when writing, it is preferable to use the active voice so as to be absolutely clear about what is meant.

John **is washing** the dog.
John **washes** the dog.

The men **were clearing** the field.
The men **cleared** the field.

Exercise
17·6

Using each of the following verbs provided, write two original sentences: one that uses the verb in the passive voice, and then one that uses the verb in the stative passive.

EXAMPLE: repair

The car is being repaired in the city.

The washing machine is repaired and ready for use.

1. ruin

   a. _____

   b. _____

2. destroy

   a. _____

   b. _____

3. paint

   a. _____

   b. _____

4. misspell

   a. _____

   b. _____

5. heal

   a. _____

   b. _____

The subjunctive mood

The English subjunctive mood has three forms. One is the infinitive of a verb with the omission of the particle word **to**: **(to) go**, **(to) be**, and so on. The second form is the past tense of a verb. In the case of the verb **to be**, only the plural past tense (**were**) is used in the subjunctive. The third form uses the auxiliary **would** followed by an infinitive or by **have** and a past participle. Let's look at these three forms:

INFINITIVE	FORM 1	FORM 2	FORM 3
to be	be	were	would be/would have been
to come	come	came	would come/would have come
to go	go	went	would go/would have gone
to speak	speak	spoke	would speak/would have spoken

The infinitive form of the subjunctive is used in sentences that convey a suggestion, a request, a recommendation, or a proposal. Note that the conjunction **that** is optional in such sentences. For example:

I suggest **she find** another way to get to work.	*not* she finds
Would you recommend that **they be** allowed to stay here?	*not* they are

The past-tense form of the subjunctive is used to express a wish or a condition and is often combined with a subjunctive clause that includes either **would** plus an infinitive or **would have** plus a past participle:

◆ A wish

> If only Jack **were** here with us now.
> If you **could** just try to understand my perspective.
> If only he **had tried** a little harder.

◆ A condition

> If the rain **let up**, we would go out for a long walk.
> My son would have been here if he **had known** that you needed help.
> If you **were** my son, I would give you the same advice.

Notice that a "wish" statement often includes the word **only**.

In a conditional statement, the **if** clause sets the condition, and the accompanying clause is the "result" if the condition is met.

condition   **result**

If she were well, she would pay us a visit.

Complete each of the following sentences with any appropriate phrase.

1. I suggest _____ .

2. No one recommended she _____ .

3. The lawyer requested it _____ .

4. The mayor proposed that _____ .

5. Would you suggest that the law _____ ?

Using the following verbs provided, write sentences that express a wish.

1. to find _____

2. to be _____

3. to be able to _____

4. to be seen _____

5. to have driven _____

*Using the following pairs of verbs provided, write sentences that express a condition and a result; include a clause that begins with **if**.*

EXAMPLE: to sing / to listen

If she sang in tune, I would listen to her song.

6. to bring / to eat

_____

7. permit / to love to chat

_____

8. have insisted / have not left

_____

9. to have to / to understand

_____

10. to be / to be

_____

Phrasal verbs

Phrasal verbs are verbs that are combined with other words—prepositions and adverbs—to form a new meaning, often a meaning that is radically different from the meaning of the verb alone. Because there are hundreds of such constructions, this chapter illustrates only a sampling of high-frequency verbs that form commonly used phrasal verbs.

common verb + adverb and/or preposition

to hold + up (to rob)

When an adverb, a preposition, or a combination of both is attached to a verb, the conjugation of the verb is not altered. It is the meaning and, therefore, the use of the verb that is changed. Let's look at the common verb **to come** to see how its meaning changes in a few phrasal verb forms:

to come to	*to regain consciousness*
to come up to	*to approach*
to come up with	*to create, or to discover*

Compare the use of these three phrasal verbs with a standard verb in the following examples:

When Jane **came to**, she didn't know where she was.
When Jane **regained consciousness**, she didn't know where she was.

I **came up to** the weary horse and patted its nose.
I **approached** the weary horse and patted its nose.

How did you **come up** with so much money?
How did you **find** so much money?

In order to deal with phrasal verbs effectively, a student of English should have a dictionary that specializes in phrasal verbs. This is an important tool for identifying phrasal verbs and for understanding their meanings and uses.

Be

Many phrasal verbs are formed from the verb **to be**. Let's look at three of them: **to be in** or **out**, **to be with it**, and **to be up to something**.

The phrasal verb **to be in**, as noted in Chapter 8, conveys that a person is at home or in the office, while **to be out** means a person is away from home or away from the office. In addition, **to be out** can indicate that someone is "out" having fun. For example:

> Little Michael **is in** for the day and taking a nap.
> What time will Dr. Schultz **be in**?
>
> Why **were** you **out** so late last night?
> My dentist **is out** for the day.

The second phrasal verb under this heading, **to be with it**, suggests fashionability or awareness of the latest trends. Used in the negative, it can mean that someone is not up to date or not in touch with pop culture.

> Andrea has another new dress. She**'s always so with it**.
> Poor Bill still can't dance. He**'s just not with it**.

To be up to something (sometimes **to be up to no good**) conveys that someone looks suspicious and has some kind of evil intentions.

> What's that man doing? I think he**'s up to something**.
> I knew you **were up to something** when I saw you holding a shovel.
> Her children **are always up to no good**.

With this phrasal verb, it is usual to follow the word **something** with an appropriate adjective; for example: **I think he's up to something illegal.** When adding an adjective in this manner, it is also possible to change **something** to **anything** when the sentence is negated: **I don't think they're up to anything wrong.**

Break

Among the phrasal verbs that can be formed with the verb **to break** are **to break down** and **to break up**. The use of the words **up** and **down** may suggest that these are opposites, but that is not the case.

The phrasal verb **to break down** has two meanings: (1) to stop working (such as in reference to a mechanical device); and (2) to give in to one's emotions or someone's demands. For example:

> How often does this computer **break down**?
> The day had been awful, and she **broke down** and cried.
> We questioned the thief for hours, and he finally **broke down** and confessed.

The phrasal verb **to break up** carries the sense of causing someone to laugh aloud. It suggests that the actions or words in question were so funny that the person could not control his or her amusement.

> Maria's joke **broke everyone up**.
> The clown's silly antics always **broke the audience up**.

The same construction has a radically different meaning and use when followed by the preposition **with**. It means that one person is ending a romantic relationship with another person: **to break up with someone**.

> After five months of dating, she knew she had **to break up with Tom**.
> He no longer loved her. It was time **to break up**.

Breeze

The phrase **to breeze through** refers to the ability to carry out a task with ease or dispatch.

> Don **breezed through** his workday and set off for his date with Tina.
> No one ever **breezes through** Professor Chang's exams.

Count

Do not confuse the usage **to count** (on)—that is, in the sense of to calculate by using one's fingers—with the phrasal verb **to count on**, which means **to rely on**. The preposition **upon** sometimes replaces **on** in the phrasal meaning.

> The little boy **counted** on his fingers.
> I know I can **count on** you for your support.
> You shouldn't have **counted on** Jim to give you any help in moving.

Exercise 18·1

Using each phrasal verb provided, write two original sentences.

EXAMPLE: to be in

Mr. Cane won't be in until after two P.M.

I have to stay in this evening and do some studying.

1. to be out

   a. _____

   b. _____

2. to be with it

   a. _____

   b. _____

3. to be up to something/no good

   a. _____

   b. _____

4. to break down

   a. _____

   b. _____

5. to break up (with)

   a. _____

   b. _____

6. to breeze through

   a. _____

   b. _____

Cut

The verb **cut** can be combined with the preposition **out**: **to cut (something) out**. Meanings of this phrasal verb include (1) to stop doing something; (2) to eliminate or cast out someone or something; and (3) to clip out or excise a shape from something. Here are some examples:

> **Cut that out!** You're being too noisy!
> Why **cut me out?** I spent as much time on the project as anyone.
> Maria **cut out a cartoon** from the newspaper.
> I'll **cut a recipe out of** the magazine.

This kind of phrasal verb is special in that the object of the verb can either precede or follow the preposition **out** if that object is a noun. Pronouns can only precede the preposition. Don't forget that prepositions in phrasal verbs can serve as adverbs:

noun direct object + preposition

I cut **an interesting article** + **out** for you.

preposition + noun direct object

I cut **out** + **an interesting article** for you.

pronoun direct object + preposition

I cut **it** + **out** for you.

This flexibility occurs with many phrasal verbs—but *not with all*. This characteristic is identified in reference to other phrasal verbs in the remainder of this chapter as the "flexible position" of a preposition. Be aware that many of these prepositions are not functioning as prepositions in these sentences; they are functioning as adverbs. In the phrasal verb **to call (someone) up**—meaning either to phone someone or to conscript someone for military service—**up** is used as an adverb. Consider the following sentence:

> They **called up my brother** to serve two years in the army.

In this sentence, the words **up my brother** do not constitute a prepositional phrase. Instead, **up** modifies the verb **call**, and **my brother** is a direct object.

Drop

When **to drop** is combined with **in**, the new phrasal verb means to stop at someone's home for a short visit. To specify what person is being visited, the preposition **on** is added. Here are some examples:

> My parents **dropped in** last night around eight.
> When you're in town, please **drop in on us**.
> I never **drop in on Michael** unexpectedly.

End

When **up** is added to the verb **to end**, the phrase takes on either of two distinct meanings: (1) to reach completion or termination; or (2) when the preposition **with** is added, to find oneself in the company of someone or in possession of something—usually a result that is unwanted or unpleasant. Let's look at some examples:

> These meetings won't **end up** until tomorrow after two P.M.
> Professor Hill **ended the lecture up with** a few words of advice.
> After her date with Jim, Maria **ended up with** a bad cold.
> I wanted to dance with Martin! How did I **end up with** Michael?

Sometimes **to end up with** is stated as **to wind up with**. They mean the same thing:

> He **ended up with** no money at all.   He **wound up with** no money at all.

The preposition in this phrasal verb has a flexible position around the object:

> She **ended up the discussion** with a little joke.
> She **ended the discussion up** with a little joke.
> She **ended it up** with a little joke.

Follow

When **to follow** is combined with **up**, and sometimes **on**, the phrasal verb means to examine something that has been done, or to evaluate how someone has performed. Some examples:

> I'll **follow up on** Maria's progress with a report.
> The detective decided to **follow up** the new clue.
> The reporter was **following up on** the strange story.

When the preposition **up** is used without **on** in this phrasal verb, **up** has a flexible position around the object:

> We should **follow that report up**.
> We should **follow up that report**.
> We should **follow it up**.

Fool

The verb **to fool** is synonymous with *to deceive*. However, when **around** is attached to the verb, new meanings emerge: (1) it means to hang about idly; (2) when the preposition **with** is added, it means to do something wasteful or useless; and (3) when used with the preposition **on** instead, it means to be unfaithful. Here are some examples:

> There was nothing else to do, so we just **fooled around** in the park.
> Why are you **fooling around with** that old radio?
> If you're **fooling around on** me, I want you to tell me now.

Get

Several phrasal verbs are formed with the verb **to get**. Two that are worth discussion are **to get away (with)** and **to get at**.

When **to get away** is used alone, it means to escape, or to move away from a location. The addition of the preposition **with** changes the meaning: the new phrase means to carry out an evil act without punishment. Look at these examples:

The prisoner dug a tunnel from his cell and tried to **get away**.
Get away from the window. It's drafty there.
He thought he **got away with** his crime, but he was arrested last week.

Get at has three meanings: (1) to put one's hands on or attack someone; (2) to hint at something; and (3) to begin discussing something. Some examples:

The bully was trying to **get at** me, but my friends held him back.
I don't understand. What are you **getting at**?
It's time we finally **get at** the heart of the matter and solve this problem.

Exercise
18·2

Complete each sentence that follows with any appropriate phrase or clause that incorporates a phrasal verb.

1. Jonathan knew he could count _____.

2. Our new neighbors like to drop _____.

3. I think it's about time to end _____.

4. I hope you can follow _____ up.

5. We learned that Helen had fooled around _____.

6. The youngsters are in the backyard fooling _____.

7. The three prisoners got _____.

8. Let's get at _____ before it gets too late.

9. She wanted a prom dress but ended up _____.

10. I don't understand. What are you getting _____?

Have

Have is another high-frequency verb that can form numerous phrasal verbs. One that bears analysis is the phrase **to have something against**. This combination of words means to harbor an attitude of disrespect or dislike. Some examples:

What do you **have against** me? I never did anything to you.
Anna **had something against** Bob and let him know it.
I **have nothing against** apple pie. I just don't want any.

Notice that with the third example, **something** changes to **nothing** in the negative. When this phrase is negated with **not**, the word **anything** is used: **I don't have anything against apple pie.**
When **have** is combined with **on** another meaning is derived. It is synonymous with **wear**. For example:

Why do you **have** that old shirt **on**?
When the postman came to the door, I didn't **have** anything **on**.
I love the blouse you gave me. I **have** it **on** right now.

Lay

The phrasal verb **to lay off** (of) has two meanings: (1) often followed by the preposition **of**, it means to stop bothering or harassing someone; (2) used without **of**, it means to end a person's employment. The latter meaning is sometimes accompanied by the preposition **from**. The following examples illustrate the variants:

> **Lay off** (of) me! You have no right talking to me like that!
> Tom just won't **lay off** (of) the man who scratched his new car.
> Business was bad, and the boss had **to lay the men off** (from their jobs).

The preposition **off** in this phrasal verb has a flexible position around the object:

> Mr. Jones **laid the whole staff off**.
> Mr. Jones **laid off the whole staff**.
> Mr. Jones **laid everyone off**.

Lead

When the verb **to lead** is followed by the preposition **on**, the phrase has the normal meaning of to continue to lead, but when a direct object is included, its meaning becomes to tantalize someone—often with the idea of love or romance. These examples shed further light:

> **Lead on**, sir. These men will follow you anywhere.
> Are you just **leading me on**? I can't believe your story is true.
> The woman was **leading Bill on**. She just wanted his money.

The preposition **on** in this phrasal verb has a flexible position around the object:

> Why are you **leading on** that nice young man?
> Why are you **leading that nice young man on**?
> Why are you **leading him on**?

Let

Combining the verb **let** with the preposition **down** yields a phrasal verb that means to disappoint someone. It can also have the meaning of to ease up in an activity. Consider these examples:

> Don't **let me down**. Please lend me the money.
> John knew he was **letting her down** when he couldn't help her move.
> Don't **let down** now. You've got only a mile left to go in the marathon.

The preposition **down** in this phrasal verb has a flexible position around the object:

> We can't **let down Uncle Bill**.
> We can't let **Uncle Bill down**.
> We can't **let him down**.

When the verb **let** is followed by **on**, the phrase means to be obvious, or to provide knowledge or information. Add the preposition **about** to cite the topic of the information. To cite the recipient of the information, add the preposition **to**. Here are some examples:

> Don't **let on** that you know me.
> You mustn't **let on to** Robert **about** the accident we had.
> She didn't **let on to** me **about** it, but I guessed the truth.

Make

The verb **to make** has a variety of uses and can form many phrasal verbs. Here, just a salient few are considered.

To make of has three primary meanings: (1) to interpret someone or something; (2) to make a success of oneself; and (3) in the construction **to make something of it**, to invite someone to fight. Here are examples:

> I don't know what **to make of** this note from Karen. What does it mean?
> John has **made something of** himself and has become rich in the process.
> Yes, I took your books! Do you want **to make something of it**?

Followed by the preposition **up**, the verb **to make** produces a few new meanings: (1) to fabricate or lie; (2) to apply cosmetics; (3) often with the pronoun **it** and using the preposition **to**, to compensate a person for something; and (4) accompanied by the preposition **with**, to reconcile.

> I confess. I **made the whole story up**.
> Two women were **making the bride up** for her wedding.
> Tom promised **to make it up to me**, but nothing ever happened.
> Robert **made up with Carmen**, but she was still angry.

The preposition **up** in this phrasal verb has a flexible position around the object:

> John **made up another excuse**.
> John **made another excuse up**.
> John **made it up**.

If you use the preposition **for** with **to make up**, the phrasal verb means to compensate for something that was done.

> I hope this check will **make up for** the problem you had with our product.
> You can't **make up for** such bad behavior.

When **to make up** is used with the object **the bed**, the reference is to putting fresh sheets and coverings on a mattress. With that meaning, the preposition **up** again has a flexible position around the object:

> Let's **make up the bed**.
> Let's **make the bed up**.
> Let's **make it up**.

Exercise 18·3

Fill in each blank in the following sentences with the appropriate form of the missing phrasal verb. Use the definition provided in parentheses to choose each verb.

EXAMPLE: The police officer came <u>up</u> to me and asked for my identification.

1. They're going _____ the entire advertising department. (end employment)

2. I hope my sister doesn't _____ that I got in at two A.M. (be obvious, provide information)

3. I can't understand why Phillip _____ you. (harbor an attitude of disrespect)

4. My boss just doesn't know what _____ this report. (interpret)

5. Although he's still angry, I finally _____ my ex-boyfriend. (become friends again)

6. Little Billy _____ a silly story about why he was late again. (fabricate)

7. All your apologies cannot _____ for the way you treated me. (compensate)

8. He can't restrain himself from _____ having bought a new house. (be obvious)

9. I wish that horrid man would just _____ me. (stop bothering)

10. I think it was cruel of you to _____ Jake _____. (tantalize with the idea of love)

Pass

When the verb **pass** is followed by **away**, a new meaning is produced: **to die**. This expression is often used in place of **to die** in order to blunt the reality and impart a tone of compassion. When the verb **pass** is followed by the phrase **off as**, the meaning of the phrasal verb is to represent that someone or something is different from what it really is. Some examples:

Old Mrs. Jarvis **passed away** last night.
The man tried to **pass the pretty girl off** as his daughter.
The crooked dealer thought he could **pass off an old chair** as an antique.

The preposition **off** in this phrasal verb has a flexible position around the object:

He **passed off a forgery** as the real thing.
He **passed a forgery off** as the real thing.
He **passed it off** as the real thing.

Set

With the addition of the preposition **back**, the verb **to set** has three new meanings: (1) followed by the preposition **from**, to move something away from other things; (2) to change the time on the clock to an earlier time; and (3) to cause a temporary failure or delay.

I **set** the stack of books **back from** my work space. I needed more room to write.
Tomorrow we have **to set all the clocks back** an hour.
The broken equipment **set us back** a whole week in completing the job.

When **to set** is followed by **off**, it has four primary new meanings: (1) to anger someone; (2) to cause something to explode or go off; (3) followed by the preposition **on**, to depart for a journey; and (4) followed by the preposition **for**, to depart for a specific destination. Some examples:

Jim's cruel remark really **set Anna off**. She began to scream at him.
The bomb was **set off** by a remote detonator.
The next morning we **set off on** the short trip to Sun Valley.
After breakfast the tourists **set off for** Las Vegas.

The preposition **off** in this phrasal verb has a flexible position around the object:

That **set off my boss**.   Who **set off the alarm**?
That **set my boss off**.   Who **set the alarm off**?
That **set him off**.   Who **set it off**?

Stand

When **to stand** is combined with **for**, the phrasal verb has two meanings: (1) to symbolize something; and (2) to tolerate something. Look at these examples:

> The American flag **stands for** freedom and democracy.
> I won't **stand for** your rude behavior any longer.

Take

When **to take** is combined with **back**, it has three meanings: (1) to return something; (2) to trigger a memory of something; and (3) to retract something.

> I **took the tools I borrowed back** to Jim.
> Hearing that song **takes me back** to when I was still in college.
> **Take that back!** You know that's not true!

The adverb **back** in this phrasal verb has a flexible position around the object:

> Mark won't **take back the money**.
> Mark won't **take the money back**.
> Mark won't **take it back**.

Another phrasal verb is formed with **to take** and the preposition **up**. It has four primary meanings: (1) to raise the hem of a garment; (2) sometimes using the preposition **with**, to discuss a subject; (3) to be involved in an activity; and (4) followed by the preposition **on**, to agree to a proposal. Here are examples of each:

> That dress is too long. **Take it up** a couple inches.
> The committee **took up** the problem of recycling plastics.
> I need **to take up** the question of Jim's employment with you.
> My daughter has **taken up** stamp collecting.
> I'd like to **take them up** on their offer to buy my house.

The preposition **up** in this phrasal verb has a flexible position around the object:

> My cousin **took up the piano**.
> My cousin **took the piano up**.
> My cousin **took it up**.

Walk

The verb **to walk** when followed by **out** means to leave, or to exit. When the preposition **on** is added, the meaning is altered: to abandon something, or to jilt someone.

> Why did you **walk out on** the last act of the play?
> I don't understand why she **walked out on** Jim. Does she have a new boyfriend?

Warm

When **to warm** is followed by **up**, it means to make something warm by placing it over a heat source, or that something is becoming warm. When the preposition **to** is added to this phrase, a different meaning results: to become comfortable with a person or situation.

> It will start **warming up** around the middle of April.
> As soon as I met Jake, I **warmed up to** him right away.
> At first I thought the idea was silly, but I soon **warmed up to** it.

Water

When you add **down** to the verb **to water**, the phrase conveys that a liquid is being diluted, or that someone's efforts are being reduced in effectiveness.

> The bartender **watered down** the whiskey to reap a few more dollars.
> If you **water down** that solution any further, it won't clean anything.
> Congress hoped to **water down** a strict old law.
> The committee **watered down** the chairman's powers.

Exercise 18·4

Write an original sentence using each of the phrasal verbs provided.

1. to pass off as _____

2. to set off _____

3. to set off for _____

4. to stand for _____

5. to take back _____

6. to take up _____

7. to walk out _____

8. to walk out on _____

9. to warm up to _____

10. to water down _____

Other parts of speech

If a phrasal verb is transitive, it can be used to form the passive voice. The verb in the phrasal verb is formed as a past participle and is introduced by the auxiliary **to be**. For example:

> The two brothers **were cut out** of the will.
> The stew still has **to be warmed up**.

Many phrasal verbs can be used as nouns. In some cases, they are combined as one word by means of a hyphen and in other instances they are written as one word.

> The children played on the floor with the **cutouts**.
> After a hard winter, we're hoping for a quick **warm-up**.

In addition, nouns and past participles formed from phrasal verbs can act as adjectives:

◆ Nouns as adjectives

> The **getaway** car was a black SUV.
> We'll present a **follow-up** report tomorrow.

◆ Participles as adjectives

The **laid-off** workers began to plan a protest.
I can't eat **watered-down** soup.

Write three versions of an original sentence for each phrasal verb provided, showing the "flexible position" of the preposition with a noun and, in your third version, with a pronoun.

EXAMPLE: to break up

His jokes always broke up his friends.

His jokes always broke his friends up.

His jokes always broke them up.

1. to break down

   a. _____

   b. _____

   c. _____

2. to follow up

   a. _____

   b. _____

   c. _____

3. to lay off

   a. _____

   b. _____

   c. _____

4. to lead on

   a. _____

   b. _____

   c. _____

5. to let down

   a. _____

   b. _____

   c. _____

6. to pass off

   a. _____

   b. _____

   c. _____

7. to set off

   a. _____

   b. _____

   c. _____

8. to warm up

   a. _____

   b. _____

   c. _____

9. to water down

   a. _____

   b. _____

   c. _____

10. to make up

   a. _____

   b. _____

   c. _____

Exercise 18·6

Fill in each blank in the sentences that follow with the missing preposition, adverb, or combination of both.

1. How could that woman just walk _____ her husband and children?

2. Ms. Fleming tried to pass herself _____ only thirty years old.

3. Judge Mills won't be _____ until ten.

4. He decided to water _____ his remarks before he gave the speech.

5. I think you should get _____ from that grumpy dog.

6. Who set _____ the bomb?

7. She doesn't like Bob. She can't warm _____ him.

8. Your child should take _____ the violin.

9. You have to find a way to make _____ these bad grades.

10. He knows all the hottest clubs. He's really _____ it.

 # Letter writing and e-mail

Although the modern world offers many advanced forms of communication, from feature-laden telephones to the Internet, people still need writing skills that can be employed in the various channels. This chapter concentrates on the formats needed for writing letters and for composing e-mails.

Letter writing

The two basic forms of letters are the *informal or friendly letter* and the *formal or business letter*. Let's first look at how these two types of letter writing affect the composition of the envelope.

For both types, the addressee's name appears in the center of the envelope, and the sender's name appears in the upper left corner. On the line below each name is the street address and then the suite or apartment number (if any). The next line contains the city, the two-letter state abbreviation, and the zip code along with the four-number extension (if known). A general rule is to spell out all words in an address other than an addressee's title. However, **apartment** and **boulevard** can be abbreviated (**Apt. / Blvd.**). Compass points that are included with an address do not require periods in their abbreviations (**NW, NE, SW,** and **SE**): 31 Jones Avenue **NW**. If the address is typed and has fewer than four lines, it is generally double-spaced. Otherwise, the address is single-spaced. If the addressee is a close friend or associate of the writer, the person's courtesy title (**Mr., Ms., Mrs.**) or professional title (e.g., **Dr.**) is sometimes omitted.

If the letter is written to someone out of the country, the country name is added on a separate line. For example:

Sender of a casual letter	Addressee
John Jones	Ms. Barbara Gordon
1825 North Campbell Road	9 Avon Crescent
Schaumburg, IL 60019-3445	Kenilworth CV7 3PQ
USA	United Kingdom

A business-size envelope is approximately four inches by ten inches and is used for formal letters but is acceptable for use with informal letters as well. Most businesses have business envelopes with the name and address of the company preprinted in the sender's position in the upper left-hand corner or, on occasion, on the flap. In addition, sometimes the name and functional title (e.g., **Director of Marketing**) of the sender appears above the company name. Compare these examples:

Sender of a business letter	Addressee
Michael Hughes, Manager	A to Z Contractors
The Mills Company	11 Dryden Road NW
1800 East Main Street	Kalamazoo, MI 49016
Cutler, AL 35044-2365	

Exercise 19·1

Combine the elements in each set of entries as they should appear in the address of an informal letter.

EXAMPLE: Illinois / Geneva / Mary Jones / 60691-4404 / 1930 Gordon Drive

Ms. Mary Jones

1930 Gordon Drive

Geneva, IL 60691-4404

1. Dallas / Henry Higgins / 1556 West Palmer Street / Texas / 75211 / Apt. 3

_____

_____

_____

2. Arizona / Tucson / 32 Fifth Street / 85701 / Margaret Rutherford

_____

_____

_____

3. Third Floor / Massachusetts / Ben Roberts / 3103 North Scott Street / Boston / 02197

_____

_____

_____

Parts of the casual letter

There are not strict rules as to what parts must be included in a casual or friendly letter. In general, the letter consists of the date, the sender's address, the salutation, the body of the letter, the closing, and the signature of the sender. If the recipient is a close friend or associate of the sender and is aware of the sender's address (which appears on the envelope), it is common to omit the sender's address here.

The various parts of this kind of letter, except for the body itself, can be adjusted left or right. Likewise, paragraph indentation is optional in a friendly letter. Consider the following example:

March 10, 2009 (*date*)

1415 North Broadway Street (*optional sender's address*)
Baltimore, MD 21212

Dear Mary, (*salutation*)

It was great to see you again last week. I really enjoyed your sister's party and had a lot of fun talking with you about old times. I guess we both miss college life. The studying, exams, and occasional boring professor were often a burden, but the great people we met and the recreational activities on campus made all the difference. You helped to make my years in college special. I'm glad we got together again at the party. I hope to see more of you.

Yours truly, (*closing*)

[Signature]

An alternative approach is to place the date and the optional sender's address at the upper right of the page.

Note that a comma follows both the salutation and the closing in a casual letter.

The closing of a friendly letter can take various forms, the choice of which depends in part on the nature of the relationship between the writer and addressee. Here are some frequently used closings:

Casual	Very friendly
Truly,	Fondly,
Truly yours,	Affectionately,
Sincerely,	With love,
Sincerely yours,	With all my love,

Exercise
19·2

*Write a casual letter to a close friend named **Mary Smith** (or another name of your choosing) to tell her of your new job and to invite her to a party.*

_____

_____

_____

_____

_____

_____

_____

Parts of the business letter

It is customary to adhere to certain rules when composing a business letter. That said, there is a contemporary tendency to relax those strictures, particularly when a businessperson is communicating regularly with another businessperson and wishes to make the relationship less structured and more cordial.

Let's take the prudent course here and walk through the rules as they are normally followed:

- A business letter should be typed and composed in the Times New Roman font, twelve point.
- The date is the first element of the business letter and is either justified left or centered on the page. In American style, the month is written out and is followed by the date, which is separated from the year by a comma: March 10, 2009.
- If preprinted letterhead is not being used, the sender's address follows after a skipped line below the date and is justified left on the page. The sender's name should not be included in this part of the letter, since it appears at the bottom. (In a less used style, the sender's address appears below the signature at the end of the letter.)
- After another skipped line below the sender's address, the recipient's name and address are entered; these lines are also justified left. The first line here is the recipient's name, which is preceded by a courtesy or professional title and is followed by the person's functional title when applicable. On the lines below are, in order, the department (if any); the company name; the street address; and the city, state, and zip code. If you are writing to someone in a foreign country, the country name is the last element of this address and should be typed in capital letters. For example:

Ms. Joanne Keller	Dr. Martin Braun
Legal Department	Werner-Versand KG
Shuster and Kane, Inc.	18 Marktplatz
1600 West Schiller Avenue	86123 Augsburg
Milwaukee, WI 53201	GERMANY

- Another line is skipped before the salutation. The salutation should usually include the same courtesy or professional title as in the address line and is followed by a colon. In a friendlier style, only the first name is used, but it is still followed by a colon (rather than a comma as with informal letters). For example:

Dear Ms. Keller:	Dear Dr. Braun:	Dear Joanne:

Again, a line is skipped between the salutation and the body of the letter. The body should be single-spaced like the other parts of the letter, except that a line is skipped between paragraphs when the text is justified left. Paragraph indentation is optional and is sometimes used when the date, closing, and signature lines are centered on the page. The three commonly used formats for a business letter are block, modified block, and indented modified block. Here are examples of each:

Block format	Modified block format	Indented modified block
Date	Date	Date
Sender's address	Sender's address	Sender's address
Recipient's address	Recipient's address	Recipient's address
Salutation	Salutation	Salutation
Body of letter	Body of letter	Body of letter
Closing	Closing	Closing
Signature	Signature	Signature
Enclosure	Enclosure	Enclosure

Note that if the writer is enclosing any documents in the business letter, it is customary to type the word **Enclosure(s)** one line below the signature line.

◆ Frequently, the writer of a business letter informs the recipient of the topic of the letter by adding a brief statement before the salutation. That statement follows the abbreviation Re: (regarding). A line is skipped before and after the statement. Here is an example of this structure:

Mr. Thomas Hanson, Vice President
Adams, Inc.
12 Victory Lane
Chicago, IL 60699

Re: Recent Software Problems

Dear Mr. Hanson:

I appreciate your quick response to my earlier problems with your firm's accounting software. The downloads you provided solved my problems. However, that solution was only temporary.

At the present time, the input of all forms of data is working correctly. However, now the simplest equations that require either addition or subtraction are providing completely inaccurate totals.

I need this software to be working properly and in the very near future. Please send a technician to my office to end this predicament.

◆ When a letter is written to no specific person at a company, the salutation is usually **Dear Sir or Madam:** or **To whom it may concern:**. These phrases are also helpful when the gender of the addressee is not clear. For instance, is **Chris Jones** a man or a woman? Is **A. J. Barrons** a man or a woman? It is considered good form to obtain the name of the appropriate person in the company to whom the letter should be directed (and to clarify the gender, as well as the correct spelling, if necessary), whenever possible, and to use that person's name in the salutation. The two *vague* salutations cited in this section should be used only when that is impossible.
◆ The closing of a business letter is traditionally a simple, respectful phrase such as the following:

     Sincerely,   Regards,   Best regards,

◆ Then four lines are skipped as a space for the signature. Below the signature is the writer's name typed out.

Combine the elements in each set that follows as they should appear in the address and salutation of a business letter.

1. The Stone Company / Denver, CO / Alice French / 3103 Scott Street / Design Department / 80211 / Chief Accountant / A Proposal for the Jenner Project

   _____

   _____

   _____

   _____

   _____

   _____

   _____

   _____

2. Manager / 1515 South Wellington Avenue / Charles Gibbs / Atlanta, GA / Kaufman Brothers Shoes / 30303

   _____

   _____

   _____

   _____

   _____

   _____

   _____

   _____

Write a business letter to the address provided, requesting information regarding resorts in Florida and cruises in the Caribbean. Include personal information: number of travelers, range of cost, age level, preferred dates of travel, required facilities, and so on.

Mr. Victor Wallace
Sunnyside Travel Agency
909 E. Culver Avenue
St. Petersburg, FL 33705

_____

_____

_____

_____

_____

_____

_____

E-mails

Messages and letters sent by *electronic mail* should follow the format of a friendly letter for recipients who are close to the writer and should follow the format of a business letter for those who are on a more formal basis. E-mail format automatically provides the date and the e-mail address of the sender, but the sender must type in the recipient's e-mail address in the line marked **To**. In the line marked **CC**, the sender types in the e-mail address(es) of anyone who should receive a *copy* of the message. Also, in the line marked **BCC**, the sender types in the e-mail address(es) of anyone who will receive a *blind copy* of the message. A blind copy means that the recipient's e-mail address will not appear in the transmission.

E-mail accounts have a function allowing the writer to store a list of e-mail addresses. When an address is needed, the writer clicks on the option **Insert Address**, or similar nomenclature, to access the list and to select the e-mail address(es) to be placed automatically in the **To** line.

In the **Subject** or **Re** field, the writer enters a phrase that summarizes the intent of the message; for example: **Mom feels better** or **Proposal for Teardown on State Street**.

E-mail formats allow the sender to access files stored on a computer and transmit them along with the main message as an **Attachment**. An attachment can be a single file or a series of files.

Most e-mail messages can be written in a variety of fonts and colors, which can be chosen from a list provided as a feature of the e-mail program. In a business e-mail, it is wise to avoid unusual fonts and elaborate changes of color or size. New Times Roman in black is always correct.

Sample e-mail

To: Jane Michaels (janem@datafirm.net)
From: William Ort (billort@datafirm.net)
Subject: Friday night
Hi, Jane.
They're going to show the Bulls game at Harold's Tap on Friday. It should be a wild game. Can you join me? I'll be there with Mary and Steve. Is 7 P.M. good for you? Hope to see you there. Let me know for sure. Thanks.
Bill

The salutation, body, and closing of an e-mail should, in most cases, resemble those elements as they appear in a friendly or business letter. In friendly and casual messages, there is a tendency to abbreviate words when possible and to make the content brief. There also is a great deal of license taken with salutations. Naturally, **Dear Bill** is an appropriate salutation, but you will also encounter **Hi, Bill** or just **Bill**. In many cases, the salutation is simply avoided.

Something similar occurs with the closing of a casual e-mail. **Sincerely** is always appropriate, but you will also see **So long** or **Bye for now** or **Later**, among other expressions. In fact, a closing might be omitted and the e-mail ended with the name of the sender. And even the sender's name can be omitted.

Except in business e-mails, there is often an attempt to incorporate the jargon used in *chat rooms*, apparently in an effort to be contemporary and casual (**LOL** or laugh out loud, for example). Employing this trend in e-mails is the option of the writer. However, an e-mail writer cannot go wrong by conforming to the rules described for friendly and business letters.

Exercise 19·5

Write an e-mail to a friend, requesting the return of a personal item and including an invitation to join you at an event.

_____

_____

_____

_____

_____

_____

_____

Write an e-mail to the manager of a company at which you have applied for a job to learn about the status of your application.

_____

_____

_____

_____

_____

_____

_____

Write an e-mail to the company that painted your house or apartment, citing a complaint with the job and specifying a course of action to remedy the situation.

_____

_____

_____

_____

_____

_____

_____

_____

Text messages

One of the most common ways people communicate today is by text messages. Text messages are also known as "Short Message Service," or SMS. Sent and received on a mobile phone or other mobile device, they tend to be rather short, to the point, and written in a casual and frequently abbreviated style. The abbreviations used in e-mails are often used in this form of communication.

No address is needed for a text message, just a correct mobile phone number, for example, 312-555-7654. Texting has become so popular that today text messages can include photographs or videos that are attached to the message. And mobile phones are so sophisticated now that they are far more than just instruments of communication. They are carriers of news, weather, games, music, movies, and sources of information. They are also a powerful resource for acquiring "apps" (applications), which provide almost instantaneous information on an enormous variety of subjects.

Here are some abbreviations used in texting. They are very popular among young people and are sometimes considered an alien language by older adults. It is a matter of personal taste whether or not you use them when you tex.

2moro	tomorrow
2nite	tonight
AEAP	as early as possible
ASL	age, sex, location
B3	blah, blah, blah
BFF	best friends forever
BM&Y	between me and you
HAK	hugs and kisses
L8R	later
LOL	laugh out loud
MoF	male or female
NC	no comment
NVM	never mind
OATUS	on a totally unrelated subject
OMW	on my way
RN	right now
SLAP	sounds like a plan
WB	welcome back
WYWH	wish you were here
XOXOXO	hugs and kisses

Exercise 19·8

Write a text message to a friend, telling him or her of a new restaurant he or she should try.

_____

_____

_____

·20·
Let's write!

You have now completed a series of exercises that have given you practice in writing sentences of various types and containing all the essential structures of the English language. That means that you are ready to be more creative.

The following writing exercises will permit you to apply what you know about sentence writing in two formats: original sentences that require the use of specified grammatical and vocabulary elements and original sentences that require a specific content. In both cases, challenge yourself to create interesting and intelligent sentences. *Do not write below your level of skill.*

Specified grammatical elements

When a grammatical element is specified for use in a sentence, the nature of that sentence is dependent upon the grammatical element. For example, specifying the future tense determines when in time an action will take place. Specifiying antonyms suggests that a comparison will be made in a sentence.

Exercise
20·1

Using each set of words and phrases provided, write an original sentence that conforms to the grammar cues in parentheses. Add as many words as necessary.

EXAMPLE: (past perfect tense) he / forget / umbrella / because / mother / sick / hospital

He had forgotten his umbrella, because he had been worried about his sick mother in the hospital.

1. (present perfect tense) girlfriend / wait / gift / birthday

   _____

2. (passive voice) customs official / fire / drunk / late

   _____

3. (past tense) when / in Washington, D.C. / interview / representative / Colorado

   _____

4. (present tense) whenever / abroad / try / language / country

_____

5. (interrogative *who*) say / defendant / guilty / fine

_____

6. (conjunction *although*) Germany / locate / near/ Denmark / Scandanavian country

_____

7. (antonym) former wife / beautiful / new girlfriend

_____

8. (passive voice) week ago / barn / burn down / lightning

_____

9. (future tense) weak / infant / struggle / health / born / infection

_____

10. (present perfect tense) behave / as if / first prize

_____

Exercise
20·2

Complete the following sentences with any appropriate phrase. Include the cue word or phrase provided in parentheses in your sentence in any appropriate form.

1. The newsman reported that _____ . (peace treaty)

2. We got our tickets _____ . (wait for)

3. Why are you talking about _____ ? (and not)

4. Tina dialed the number, _____ . (hang up)

5. What do you have against _____ ? (save money)

6. I undress, take a quick shower, _____ . (as fast as)

7. Oh, _____ . (costume)

8. _____ although we had a terrible argument. (each other)

9. Whose fault _____ ? (she had an accident)

10. In 1455 Gutenberg _____ . (invention)

Fill in the blanks with appropriate phrases to form complete sentences; use the tense provided in parentheses.

EXAMPLE: (past) <u>Your daughter was</u> diligent, but <u>your son was quite lazy.</u>

1. (present) _____ just as expensive as _____ .

2. (past) _____ much sharper _____ .

3. (future) _____ jump farther _____ .

4. (present) _____ not valuable but _____ .

5. (present perfect) Either _____ or _____ .

6. (present) _____ the shortest route _____ ?

7. (past) _____ one of the least likely _____ .

8. (present) Here, _____ .

9. (present perfect) _____ finished, or _____ ?

10. (present) I myself _____ rather than _____ .

Specific content

Now it's time to write completely original sentences without conforming to a paradigm or in response to cues. The only suggestions you need to follow are the topics provided for your writing. Be sure to challenge yourself. Do not take the easy road, because having come this far in this book, you're ready for some real writing.

Write a paragraph that describes the home in which you live. You can cite such aspects as its size, the rooms, the furniture, your family, decorations, activities, and even holidays you celebrate.

_____

_____

_____

_____

_____

_____

_____

_____

Exercise 20·5

Write a paragraph that describes the schools you attended, favorite teachers and subjects, friends you made, activities in which you participated, degrees you have earned, and how you hope to apply your education to your career.

_____

_____

_____

_____

_____

_____

_____

Exercise 20·6

Write a paragraph that describes the plot of a book or the content of an article that you have recently read.

_____

_____

_____

_____

_____

_____

_____

_____

Write your autobiography: My Life So Far.

_____

_____

_____

_____

_____

_____

_____

_____

_____

Progress Check

The following items will help you understand the progress you have made while using this book. It is not meant to evaluate how much you know but rather how much you have improved. When you discover an error while checking your progress, correct it and move on. As a non-native speaker of English, you will occasionally make an error—no matter how proficient and well-studied you are—unless, of course, you spend a considerable amount of time in an English-speaking country.

   If at the end of this Progress Check you find that you have not developed as much as you wanted in a specific area, return to the chapter that covers that material and practice with it again.

Exercise 21·1

Circle the letter of the word or phrase that best completes each sentence.

1. The women are _____ to prepare a big supper for the children.

   a. cook

   b. cooked

   c. try

   d. trying

2. She _____ her new job after only one day.

   a. quit

   b. find

   c. was looking

   d. remained

3. _____ , Martin finally felt well enough to join the others in the family room.

   a. After a long nap

   b. Incredible

   c. Tomorrow morning

   d. Having nothing

4. Is Bob _____ to understand all these questions?

   a. will

   b. won't

   c. able

   d. can

5. _____ you had enough to eat?

   a. Did

   b. Have

   c. Will

   d. Shall

6. _____ you play the radio so loudly?

   a. Should have

   b. Does

   c. Haven't

   d. Must

7. _____ will Aunt Sara arrive home from England?

   a. Where

   b. Why not

   c. When

   d. From what

8. _____ the concert supposed to start at eight P.M.?

   a. Was

   b. Has been

   c. When

   d. Who is

9. _____ was the cottage on the hill covered in?

   a. Yes, the entire cottage.

   b. No, only the northern wall.

   c. With what kind of siding

   d. Where

10. _____ send me the twenty dollars by Western Union.

    a. Let

    b. Please

    c. Why don't I

    d. Whenever

11. _____ getting up early and taking a walk with me?

    a. Why

    b. Please

    c. Let's

    d. How about

12. He seemed like an honest man, _____ .

    a. yet I always had some doubts

    b. nor do I trust him

    c. for I don't have to explain why

    d. and hoping to become wealthy

13. It is either Janet or her girlfriends who _____ to go to State University.

    a. want

    b. cannot

    c. wants

    d. has

14. You can live here _____ you continue to work in our store.

    a. that

    b. wherever

    c. how

    d. as long as

15. While I was asleep on the sofa, _____ .

    a. the children run into the kitchen

    b. my mother dropped a frying pan on the floor

    c. I dream about my girlfriend

    d. we will have plenty of time later

16. The boys were camped by the river, but the wind blew _____ tent down.

    a. his

    b. their

    c. of them

    d. of theirs

17. Dr. Mills, _____ , is going to Johns Hopkins.

    a. which is very talented

    b. to whom Dr. Mills sent it

    c. has had a wonderful medical practice

    d. who is a brilliant surgeon

18. Is _____ the only way you know how to earn money?

    a. those antique vases

    b. your

    c. this

    d. steals from an old woman

19. _____ believe that John is the one who sent you that letter.

    a. She

    b. Mrs. Jacobson

    c. I myself

    d. You and me

20. Marianne received a present _____ her Aunt Vera.

    a. to

    b. from

    c. in case of

    d. till

21. The witness had no knowledge _____ the accident.

    a. for

    b. besides

    c. despite

    d. of

22. Mr. Garcia is a bit older _____ .

    a. than his wife

    b. of all the employees

    c. because of you

    d. about Mr. Miller

23. The _____ child sat in a corner and wept.

    a. afraid

    b. unable

    c. likely

    d. sad

24. Who is _____ man standing next to Maria?

    a. a

    b. an

    c. the

    d. those

25. My new car is a Chevy; _____ is a Cadillac.

    a. you

    b. hers

    c. our

    d. their

Exercise

21·2

Circle the letter of the word or phrase that best completes each sentence.

1. The _____ ceremony lasted two hours.

    a. graduation

    b. married

    c. relatives

    d. to be praised

2. The scientist studied the strange specimen _____ than usual.

    a. softer

    b. badly

    c. more carefully

    d. during the examination

3. The elderly man had become _____ ill.

    a. profoundly

    b. usually

    c. after the arrival of the doctor

    d. last month

4. The cabin was located _____ .

    a. the dark and damp forest

    b. beyond the rushing river

    c. anywhere else

    d. definitely upstairs

5. _____ , Mrs. Keller had a little fender-bender on Elm Street.

    a. Delivered tomorrow

    b. Driving home from work

    c. Having been hidden

    d. A frightening evening

6. Jack had the engagement ring _____ .

    a. hidden in his jacket pocket

    b. found the night before

    c. bought after weeks of saving

    d. being stored in his dresser

7. The _____ article was full of errors.

    a. carelessly written

    b. reading the entire statement

    c. being quickly edited

    d. developing a fever

8. The car _____ belongs to Mr. Lopez.

    a. crushed by a falling tree

    b. vigorously rushing

    c. raced around a corner

    d. merely parking across the street

9. To die _____ was the knight's only wish.

    a. for his king and country

    b. Europe is a dream of mine, too

    c. of the beautiful maiden

    d. the future battle with the enemy

10. To earn a bachelor's degree _____ .

    a. will be my next goal

    b. become a citizen

    c. make him smarter and more confident

    d. must start immediately

11. His suggestion, _____ , was considered foolish.

    a. be on time every day

    b. having been in the army

    c. to rent a limousine for the prom

    d. being at the end of his patience

12. The policeman telephoned _____ .

    a. the car would be stolen

    b. up to the girl in the back yard

    c. we stay in the house

    d. to invite us to the party

13. The only choice left was _____ .

    a. paid for the hotel room and go home

    b. stayed with the sick woman till the doctor came

    c. to the north down Main Street

    d. to remain in the cabin till the storm was over

14. _____ is still very popular with young people.

    a. Buy the latest music

    b. Dancing

    c. Having had hobbies

    d. To Florida for vacation

15. My father was determined to avoid _____ .

    a. having an accident

    b. wear a new business suit

    c. bought mother a necklace

    d. buy her something she hated

16. Their family is _____ in Canada.

    a. having been happy

    b. taking a long vacation

    c. to be tired of living

    d. employing

17. My brother often hated _____ .

    a. being the youngest in the family

    b. he had to get a job

    c. continued living in the basement

    d. be so tall

18. Jack is so funny. He's a _____ .

    a. lonely person

    b. real card

    c. hot air

    d. pulling my leg

19. That's unbelievable. Actually, your story sounds _____ to me.

    a. fishy

    b. beeline

    c. well off

    d. from scratch

20. I was happy to learn that Mary and Tom _____ .

    a. on the go

    b. are a lot of red tape

    c. in a lot of hot water

    d. are in the family way

21. I think you better start counting _____ .

    a. under his breath

    b. about

    c. from scratch

    d. to the dogs

22. _____ , the police found the wallet you lost last week.

    a. By the way

    b. At all

    c. You should have gone

    d. I wouldn't mind

23. "Thanks so much for all your help."

    "Please, _____ ."

    a. for heaven's sake

    b. don't mention it

    c. Obviously

    d. Outstanding

24. _____ ! That really hurts!

    a. Now

    b. Ouch

    c. Great

    d. Bravo

25. _____ ? That's a lie! Mary is lying!

    a. Ah

    b. What

    c. Hurrah

    d. Not at all

Circle the letter of the word or phrase that best completes each sentence.

1. I don't always snore. I _____ snore.

   a. never

   b. below

   c. none

   d. after

2. John said the woman was ugly, but I thought she was _____ .

   a. old

   b. late

   c. above

   d. beautiful

3. The clown had a sad face, but he really was always _____ .

   a. cheerful

   b. abundant

   c. sober

   d. graceful

4. He said meeting her today was accidental, but she knew it was _____ .

   a. clumsy

   b. intentional

   c. separate

   d. straight

5. I don't understand why he _____ that awful movie.

   a. repaired

   b. recommended

   c. praising

   d. would present

6. A moat _____ around the entire castle.

   a. will be spent

   b. went swimming

   c. has been given

   d. was built

7. The reporter was _____ the street fight.

   a. filmed

   b. taking

   c. photographing

   d. taken pictures

8. The band _____ by Mr. Gonzalez.

   a. was led

   b. are believed

   c. is playing too loudly

   d. have been reported

9. It _____ that the family would share in the inheritance.

   a. widely believed

   b. remarked

   c. will be strange

   d. was understood

10. They _____ the man's broken arm.

    a. were examining

    b. have been found

    c. are reported

    d. were beaten

11. _____ was given some money for a good meal.

    a. His children

    b. By a generous man

    c. The hungry woman

    d. The poor men

12. A diamond ring was given _____ by her fiancé.

    a. from Maria

    b. to her

    c. from them

    d. by Michael

13. He was being _____ the new museum.

    a. shown around

    b. presented

    c. accompanied

    d. also bring along

14. Mrs. Keller _____ invited to the anniversary party.

    a. should have

    b. liked it

    c. are being

    d. wants to be

15. The news conference _____ postponed.

    a. will have

    b. must have

    c. has to be

    d. it was mentioned

16. The other athletes aren't _____ by professionals.

    a. being

    b. be advised

    c. been instructed

    d. being trained

17. None of the passengers _____ rescued.

    a. had to be

    b. should have

    c. could not

    d. must have

18. He suggested she _____ another way to get to work.

    a. lets her

    b. goes

    c. find

    d. makes

19. If Thomas were feeling well, _____ .

    a. he can visit us tomorrow

    b. he could drive out into the country for a picnic

    c. he likes being on the team

    d. he takes his wife out to dinner again

20. If Tom could play the guitar better, I _____ to his song.

    a. can try to play

    b. don't care about

    c. will be interested

    d. would listen

21. How did you ever come _____ such a great idea?

    a. up with

    b. to

    c. around

    d. up to

22. What time will Professor Smith _____ ?

    a. break up

    b. is up

    c. breezes through

    d. be in

23. Don't worry. I'll help you out. You can _____ me.

    a. follow up

    b. count on

    c. end it up

    d. cut it out

24. Dear Jean,

Thank you for the great party. I'll see you at work tomorrow.

_____ ,

James

    a. Dear Sir

    b. Yours truly

    c. To whom it may concern

    d. jameswilson@datafirm.net

25. The newspaper reported that _____ .

   a. mentioned the injuries from the awful accident

   b. several students from the local college

   c. although the foreign tourists suffered no injuries

   d. the struggle between two local tribes continues

Answer key

1 Declarative sentences and word order

1·1 1. a. Thomas finds the wallet. b. Thomas has found the wallet. c. Thomas had found the wallet. d. Thomas will find the wallet. 2. a. The men were trying to raze the barn. b. The men have been trying to raze the barn. c. The men had been trying to raze the barn. d. The men will be trying to raze the barn. 3. a. They drop by at two P.M. b. They dropped by at two P.M. c. They have dropped by at two P.M. d. They had dropped by at two P.M. 4. a. She is working here as a counselor. b. She was working here as a counselor. c. She had been working here as a counselor. d. She will be working here as a counselor. 5. a. I had no time. b. I have had no time. c. I had had no time. d. I will have no time. 6. a. The wealthy couple travels the world on their yacht. b. The wealthy couple traveled the world on their yacht. c. The wealthy couple has traveled the world on their yacht. d. The wealthy couple will travel the world on their yacht.

1·2 *Sample answers are provided for numbers* 1 *through* 10. 1. The attorneys drew up the contracts for the merger. 2. I will cook a turkey. 3. The boys will sleep in the little room in the attic. 4. I have hoped for a long time to have a visit from you. 5. They had sat on the porch for a long time. 6. We shall be working even harder. 7. They were traveling to Greece when Erika became ill. 8. She was crying when he left. 9. Bill and I are playing catch in the backyard. 10. I am hoping the two boys will finally pass the test.

1·3 1. present 2. past 3. past 4. past 5. past 6. present 7. past 8. past 9. future 10. future

1·4 *Sample answers are provided.* 1. They apply for jobs at the same company. 2. He is suggesting you find somewhere else to live. 3. That young man has been annoying me since I arrived. 4. I will remain your friend forever. 5. He was attempting to jump to another branch when he fell from the tree. 6. He has tricked them for the last time. 7. He rubbed her shoulders gently. 8. He will be earning more than six figures. 9. The peasants had harvested the last of the fall crops. 10. I have been lending you money for years.

1·5 *Sample answers are provided.* 1. a. every other day. b. regularly. 2. a. with the car salesman. b. on the phone. 3. a. our house. b. his old computer. 4. a. his girlfriend a valentine. b. them another invitation. 5. a. well groomed. b. confident. 6. a. slowly through the village. b. the children to school today. 7. a. all afternoon. b. carelessly. 8. a. after the ball game. b. in a bar. 9. a. your nephew a lift to the station. b. her some money. 10. a. up to the old church. b. across the plaza and into a house.

1·6 *Sample answers are provided.* 1. a. On Friday b. During a thunderstorm, c. Last night d. At nine P.M. 2. a. Without thinking of the consequences, b. In Europe c. Yesterday d. Occasionally, 3. a. Finally, b. Last week c. Due to the fight, d. Soon after, 4. a. After breakfast b. On Monday c. Next week d. Tomorrow 5. a. A year ago b. Because of an earthquake, c. During the hurricane d. Recently 6. a. Although it took him a month, b. With a lot of patience and understanding from his parents, c. After meeting three boys his age, d. When he was invited to join the school's baseball team,

1·7 1. John couldn't take anyone's advice. 2. I won't accept anything but excellence. 3. There isn't anywhere for you to hide. 4. Ms. Brooks didn't speak with anybody about the problem. 5. You shouldn't give anyone so young that kind of responsibility. 6. That won't take any time at all. 7. There wasn't anything left for the little children. 8. There wasn't anyone for him to turn to. 9. My parents hadn't found any place to spend the night. 10. They won't achieve anything from their efforts.

2 Interrogative sentences

1. a. Are you home for the holidays? b. Were you home for the holidays? c. Have you been home for the holidays? 2. a. Does the arsonist burn down the bank? b. Has the arsonist burned down the bank? c. Will the arsonist burn down the bank? 3. a. Do you have to spend a lot of time studying? b. Did you have to spend a lot of time studying? c. Will you have to spend a lot of time studying? 4. a. Do the workers do the job right? b. Did the workers do the job right? c. Will the workers do the job right? 5. a. Could you really predict the outcome of the election? b. Have you really been able to predict the outcome of the election? c. Will you really be able to predict the outcome of the election?

2·2 *Sample answers are provided.* 1. Shouldn't you have been a little more polite to him? 2. Must you play your drums so late at night? 3. Won't Ms. Anderson want to meet the author, too? 4. Does that woman have to smoke so much? 5. Will you have another cup of tea? *or* Will you have arrived by Friday? 6. Is the parking attendant able to drive a stick shift? 7. Will the others join us for dinner tonight? 8. Ought he to have been so mean to her? 9. Would you take a job in another part of the country? 10. Have you ever had to study so hard before?

2·3 *Sample answers are provided.* 1. a. Did Tom really spend more than a hundred dollars? b. Did Tom really have to spend more than a hundred dollars? 2. a. Have they arrived in the capital on time? b. Have they been able to arrive in the capital on time? 3. a. Did the scientist finally develop a new method? b. Could the scientist finally develop a new method? 4. a. Do the children try to remain calm? b. Should the children try to remain calm? 5. a. Do you sometimes consider the danger involved in this? b. Shouldn't you sometimes consider the danger involved in this? 6. a. Do the second-graders spell accurately? b. Can the second-graders spell accurately? 7. a. Will Maria prepare some lunch? b. Will Maria try to prepare some lunch? 8. a. Did the judge suggest a solution? b. Did the judge want to suggest a solution? 9. a. Will they flee the storm? b. Will they be able to flee the storm? 10. a. Does he always pretend nothing is wrong? b. Must he always pretend nothing is wrong?

2·4 1. a. Did a plumber fix the leaking pipes? b. Was a plumber fixing the leaking pipes? 2. a. Couldn't you work on that old car? b. Couldn't you be working on that old car? 3. a. Have the judges spoken about this for a long time? b. Have the judges been speaking about this for a long time? 4. a. Does time go by very fast? b. Is time going by very fast? 5. a. Did thunder roll across the foothills? b. Was thunder rolling across the foothills? 6. a. Will you take a series of exams? b. Will you be taking a series of exams? 7. a. Has Mr. Kelly wanted to vacation there? b. Has Mr. Kelly been wanting to vacation there? 8. a. Is he crazy? b. Is he being crazy? 9. a. Have the revelers had a good time at the celebration? b. Have the revelers been having a good time at the celebration? 10. a. Should I sit nearer to her? b. Should I be sitting nearer to her?

2·5 1. What did the attendant close and lock at seven sharp? 2. When do they leave for Puerto Rico? 3. What isn't always easy to understand? 4. Whose two puppies got their shots today? 5. From whom did they probably catch the flu? 6. How do we plan on getting to the match? 7. Where did that big bully throw the ball? 8. When should the girls come home? 9. With which boy will Andrea dance? 10. Why do they know about the change in plans?

2·6 *Sample answers are provided.* 1. Why do you always contradict me? 2. How do you spell the applicant's last name? 3. With whom was the young man arguing? 4. Which airline flies directly to Frankfurt? 5. When did you decide to become a physician?

2·7 *Sample answers are provided.* 1. a. How little were the newborn pups? b. Each of the pups weighed less than eight ounces. 2. a. How large is the mayor's new house? b. The mayor's new house is a gigantic mansion. 3. a. How frequently do you get an oil change? b. I get an oil change every four thousand miles. 4. a. How difficult did you find the GRE? b. I found the GRE less challenging than I expected. 5. a. How hot was it in Miami yesterday? b. It was over ninety-five degrees yesterday. 6. a. How strong must a person be to become a mountain climber? b. A person should be in good condition and have a developed body to become a mountain climber. 7. a. How often do you travel abroad? b. I travel abroad about two times a year. 8. How did the worker carry the dynamite? The worker carried the dynamite carefully. 9. How many of the children went to the zoo? Most of the children went to the zoo. 10. How did John work today? John worked lazily today.

3 Questions and answers

3·1 *Sample answers are provided.* 1. a. Did the conductor of the orchestra study music in New York? b. Yes, the conductor of the orchestra studied music in New York. c. No, the conductor of the orchestra didn't study music in New York. He studied music in Berlin. 2. a. Did the discovery of the New World change the world forever? b. Yes, the discovery of the New World changed the world forever. c. No, the discovery of the New World didn't change the world forever. However, it gave the world new knowledge about our planet. 3. a. Are there numerous species of birds of prey in this region? b. Yes, there are numerous species of birds of prey in this region. c. No, there aren't numerous species of birds of prey in this region. There are only two species of birds of prey in this region. 4. a. Did the hatchlings suffer during the cold weather? b. Yes, the hatchlings suffered during the cold weather. c. No, the hatchlings didn't suffer during the cold weather. The hatchlings were kept in a heated coop. 5. a. Did your cousin in Cleveland win the lottery? b. Yes, my cousin in Cleveland won the lottery. c. No, my cousin in Cleveland didn't win the lottery. He won a new car. 6. a. Is the performance supposed to start at eight P.M.? b. Yes, the performance is supposed to start at eight P.M. c. No, the performance isn't supposed to start at eight P.M. It's supposed to start at nine P.M.   7. a. Was the operation a total success? b. Yes, the operation was a total success. c. No, the operation wasn't a total success. The patient died on the operating table.   8. a. Does Mr. Keller's niece have great artistic ability? b. Yes, Mr. Keller's niece has great artistic ability. c. No, Mr. Keller's niece doesn't have great artistic ability. She has great musical ability.   9. a. Are outdoor concerts given on Mondays and Fridays? b. Yes, outdoor concerts are given on Mondays and Fridays. c. No, outdoor concerts aren't given on Mondays and Fridays. They're given on Tuesdays and Fridays.   10. a. Did the toddler fall asleep on the floor? b. Yes, the toddler fell asleep on the floor. c. No, the toddler didn't fall asleep on the floor. He fell asleep in his father's lap.

3·2 *Sample answers are provided.*   1. a. Who arrived in time for the dedication? b. When did the men from the home office arrive for the dedication? c. What did the men from the home office arrive in time for?   2. a. Which bull became enraged and charged the unsuspecting visitors? b. What did the old bull do? c. Whom did the old bull charge? 3. a. When did several tourists lose their way in a dangerous blizzard? b. In the winter of 2008, how many tourists lost their way in a dangerous blizzard? c. In the winter of 2008, who lost their way in a dangerous blizzard?   4. a. Who was berated mercilessly by the angry judge? b. How was the defendant berated by the angry judge? c. By whom was the defendant mercilessly berated?   5. a. Which hunter bought some shells before heading out to the duck blind? b. What did the eager hunter buy before heading out to the duck blind? c. When did the eager hunter buy some shells?

3·3 *Sample answers are provided.*   1. a. The woman constantly thought about the problems she was having with her neighbors. b. With whom was the woman having problems? c. What did the woman constantly think about?   2. a. I bravely jumped into the swirling river and tried to swim to the opposite shore. b. What did I bravely jump into? c. To which shore did I try to swim?   3. a. No one in our department suspected those men of having committed crimes in another state. b. What did no one suspect? c. Where did those men commit their crimes?   4. a. The children performed folk songs and dances that delighted the foreign guests. b. What kind of songs and dances did the children perform? c. What delighted the foreign guests?   5. a. Some nocturnal animals prey on small rabbits and mice. b. What kind of animals prey on small rabbits and mice? c. What do some nocturnal animals prey on?

3·4 *Sample answers are provided.*   1. The new restaurant is closed on Mondays.   2. The price of that DVD player is going to be more than a hundred dollars.   3. The treasure was buried in a large metal chest.   4. Ms. Burns had that horrible argument with the new department manager.   5. We want to leave for the game at about one thirty. 6. The lecturer was speaking about the troubles in Iraq.   7. I want to go to Europe on vacation next year. 8. You can always rely on me in times like this.   9. I plan on leaving for work right after breakfast. 10. The children had to live at a relative's house.

3·5 *Sample answers are provided.*   1. a. Mary recently told me that she wanted to break up. b. When did Mary tell you that she wanted to break up?   2. a. Some of the students volunteered at a day camp during summer vacation. b. When did some of the students volunteer at a day camp?   3. a. My grandfather travels to New England every autumn. b. Where does your grandfather travel every autumn?   4. a. Winter hiking in the Colorado Rockies is dangerous. b. Where is winter hiking dangerous?   5. a. Their cottage is located in the woods near Lake Michigan. b. Near what lake is their cottage in the woods located?   6. a. Mr. Newman's niece is getting married on Saturday. b. Whose niece is getting married on Saturday?   7. a. I seldom speak to my mother-in-law anymore. b. How often do you speak to your mother-in-law?   8. a. The boy is growing so much that he'll soon be as tall as a tree. b. How tall is the growing boy going to be?   9. a. I went hunting or fishing every day while visiting Canada. b. When did you go hunting and fishing every day?   10. a. The extremely beautiful girl on the left is the winner from Puerto Rico. b. What kind of girl is the winner from Puerto Rico?

3·6 *Sample answers are provided.*   1. Based on my work schedule, I can have this project completed by the end of the month.   2. At the very least, their two plans differ in cost.   3. The dissertation of a graduate student from Boston was rejected as incompetent.   4. This year's marathon course is twenty-four miles long, with obstacles located every six miles.   5. The Battle of the Bulge took place during World War II after the enemy launched an unexpected counterattack.   6. The young woman who wrote this beautiful letter perished at sea in a terrible storm. 7. She always contradicts you because she thinks that her ideas are perfect.   8. The beautiful actress in this play is from Italy.   9. I can't believe you because you've told me nothing but lies and half-truths.   10. No, I met him recently, but I feel I can trust his sincerity.

4 Imperatives

4·1 *Sample answers are provided.*   1. Keep away from me!   2. Give me that!   3. Get out!   4. Don't be a jerk! 5. Hurry up!   6. Leave me alone!   7. Don't excite the dog!   8. Hang on tight!   9. Pour me a Coke! 10. Have a heart!

4·2 *Sample answers are provided.*   1. a. Please enjoy the rest of the trip. b. Enjoy the rest of the trip, please.   2. a. Please find the capital of Ireland on the map. b. Find the capital of Ireland on the map, please.   3. a. Please remember to take your receipt. b. Remember to take your receipt, please.   4. a. Please choose a partner for the rumba. b. Choose a partner for the rumba, please.   5. a. Please explain this sentence to me. b. Explain this sentence to me, please. 6. a. Please remain in your assigned seats. b. Remain in your assigned seats, please.   7. a. Please pretend that none of this happened. b. Pretend that none of this happened, please.   8. a. Please join in the fun. b. Join in the fun, please.

9. a. Please follow my instructions. b. Follow my instructions, please.   10. a. Please hurry down to dinner. b. Hurry down to dinner, please.

4·3 *Sample answers are provided.*   1. a. Let's spend about two hundred dollars. b. Let the girls spend about two hundred dollars.   2. a. Let's send Jim a text. b. Let Maria send Jim a text.   3. a. Let's send them another e-mail. b. Let the boss send them another e-mail.   4. a. Let's report the burglary to the police. b. Let Mr. Snyder report the burglary to the police.   5. a. Let's repair the rickety steps. b. Let the boys repair the rickety steps.   6. a. Let's try to signal the boat struggling in the swift current. b. Let Captain Jones try to signal the boat struggling in the swift current.   7. a. Let's send for the paramedics. b. Let my wife send for the paramedics.   8. a. Let's drive to the edge of the cliff. b. Let the stuntman drive to the edge of the cliff.   9. a. Let's put up a privacy fence. b. Let the neighbors put up a privacy fence.   10. a. Let's solve the difficult equation. b. Let John solve the difficult equation.

4·4 1. a. How about sitting down under a shady tree? b. Why don't you sit down under a shady tree? c. Why don't we sit down under a shady tree?   2. a. How about coming to an understanding about this matter? b. Why don't you come to an understanding about this matter? c. Why don't we to come to an understanding about this matter?   3. a. How about letting them work it out for themselves? b. Why don't you let them work it out for themselves? c. Why don't we let them work it out for themselves?   4. a. How about granting her permission to take the trip? b. Why don't you grant her permission to take the trip? c. Why don't we grant her permission to take the trip?   5. a. How about singing a song for Grandma? b. Why don't you sing a song for Grandma? c. Why don't we sing a song for Grandma?   6. a. How about refraining from using such language? b. Why don't you refrain from using such language? c. Why don't we refrain from using such language?   7. a. How about fertilizing the fields with dung? b. Why don't you fertilize the fields with dung? c. Why don't we fertilize the fields with dung?   8. a. How about opening a business on State Street? b. Why don't you open a business on State Street? c. Why don't we open a business on State Street?   9. a. How about registering to vote in the next election? b. Why don't you register to vote in the next election? c. Why don't we register to vote in the next election?   10. a. How about trying to behave a little better? b. Why don't you try to behave a little better? c. Why don't we try to behave a little better?

4·5 *Sample answers are provided.*   1. Please pass me the butter.   2. Let's get together and play poker tomorrow night.   3. Let the boys take a couple laps around the track to warm up.   4. Please, refrain from chatting so others can concentrate on their studies!   5. How about helping me translate this article into English?   6. Why don't you find a good job and settle down?   7. Why don't we spend more time with the children?   8. Let's work out together at the gym tomorrow.   9. Please keep your dog on a leash.   10. Why don't you fax a copy of the contract to me?

5 Coordinating and correlative conjunctions

5·1 *Sample answers are provided.*   1. a. During last year's vacation, we spent time at the seashore, and we went snorkeling with the beautiful fish in the bay. b. During last year's vacation, we spent time at the seashore and went snorkeling with the beautiful fish in the bay.   2. a. I wanted to attend the reception for the young candidate, but I became ill and had to stay home. b. I wanted to attend the reception for the young candidate but became ill and had to stay home.   3. a. Should we stay here in the city, or should we travel to Mexico to visit our relatives? b. Should we stay here in the city or travel to Mexico to visit our relatives?   4. a. She does not care for his ideas about the economy, nor does she trust his judgment about it. b. She neither cares for his ideas about the economy nor trusts his judgment about it.   5. a. She told lies about me, and she ruined my friendship with Jack. b. She told lies about me and ruined my friendship with Jack.   6. a. Mr. Brown had concerns about your lack of skill and maturity, yet he gave you an opportunity to work here. b. Mr. Brown had concerns about your lack of skill and maturity, yet gave you an opportunity to work here.   7. a. She looked beautiful in the silk dress, but she wasn't satisfied with her hair. b. She looked beautiful in the silk dress but wasn't satisfied with her hair.

5·2 *Sample answers are provided.*   1. all negotiations failed.   2. do you have to stay in Chicago on business?   3. life in the desert was meant for rattlers and not men.   4. I'm sending you to the Denver office.   5. I continue to feel that she is undeserving of it.   6. There was the sound of rolling thunder in the western hills   7. We're going to have to start budgeting   8. You shouldn't make so many excuses for yourself   9. He had a good track record in finance   10. You seem confident enough to handle the job

5·3 *Sample answers are provided.*   1. Will you be able to go to the concert, or are you still not feeling well?   2. Neither Mike nor Jim has any interest in the new girl.   3. I really can't help you, for I have no knowledge of the subject.   4. The mall was closed, so we went to a movie.   5. She's a very arrogant woman, yet there's something quite appealing about her.

5·4 *Sample answers are provided.*   1. she is clever   2. plan to enter graduate school in the fall   3. than I heard her screams out on the street   4. stop staying out so late   5. then I will have to punish my son   6. Maria burst into tears   10. I have neither any knowledge

5·5 *Sample answers are provided.*   1. Maria wants to become either a correspondent or a diplomat.   2. Neither his concerti nor his sonatas are as famous as his symphonies.   3. If our two countries attend the peace conference, then war can be avoided.   4. Their account is not only unethical but also rather careless.   5. The plumber had hardly crawled into the attic space, when the roof began to sag.   6. Both Maria and Nina like the handsome, new manager.   7. Have you decided whether to go out tonight or to study?   8. She had scarcely lain down in her tent, when she heard the hissing of a snake.   9. I would rather stand up for what I believe in than run away.   10. No sooner had I stepped into the clearing than I saw the bear.

5·6   *Sample answers are provided.*1. Algebra and geometry are my favorite subjects.   2. You can play in the basement, but try to be quiet.   3. We're all glad to see you, for you're the only one who can solve this problem.   4. You haven't paid rent in four months, so I think it's time to pack your things and leave.   5. You can have either a piece of pie or a piece of cake.   6. You're not only a foolish man but also a cruel man.   7. No sooner had he opened the cage than the snake struck.   8. Would she really rather sit alone than sit with the group?   9. Scarcely had John come back home, when several friends showed up.   10. If you had been on time, (then) you wouldn't have missed the test.

6   Subordinating conjunctions and conjunctive adverbs

6·1   *Sample answers are provided.*   1. Tom startled Mary with a loud scream   2. I know you're going to marry another woman   3. you continue to tell us the truth   4. we accept you into the program   5. you eventually decide to settle down   6. we're on the verge of divorce   7. you apologize to my parents   8. her GRE is good   9. the girls are finished with their game   10. you arrived here last month

6·2   *Sample answers are provided.*   1. you take your shower / While you take your shower, I'm going to make some breakfast.   2. she gets to San Francisco / Whenever she gets to San Francisco, she always visits the museums.   3. she continued to act so arrogantly / As long as the witness continued to act so arrogantly, the jurors couldn't believe her.   4. I unload the dishwasher / After I unload the dishwasher, can you set the table for me?   5. he had found a good job / Now that he had found a good job, his mother was less concerned about him.   6. their relationship grew worse / Before their relationship grew worse, they resolved the problem.   7. he received his first paycheck / Once John received his first paycheck, he opened a savings account.   8. you can prove that you're of age / Assuming that you can prove that you're of age, you will receive your inheritance.   9. they finally learn their lines. / Unless they learn their lines, the young actors will be fired.   10. you finish your homework / Until you finish your homework, you can't watch television.

6·3   *Sample answers are provided.*   1. Even though we could still hear thunder in the distance   2. When Hank finished his studies in Brussels   3. Inasmuch as you lied to me   4. After sighting the approaching storm   5. Once people learn of the maid's criminal record   6. Before Jake became a football hero   7. If you don't study hard now   8. After she proves that she had good credit   9. although we have almost no more money   10. although it was a pleasant kind of fatigue

6·4   *Sample answers are provided.*   1. Thomas usually spends a lot of time in a museum whenever he visits Rome.   2. As long as you behave yourself, you can stay in the living room with the adults.   3. She speaks as if she were the one who won the prize.   4. Assuming that you're still in town, I'd like to take you out to dinner.   5. It's cold, of course, because it's winter.   6. She sat on the bench where she first met George.   7. I let him play video games in order that he develop hand-eye coordination.   8. Since we moved to Seattle, we've had a hard time adjusting to the climate.   9. Since you gave him a black eye, it's up to you to apologize.   10. I don't understand how she got so ill.

6·5   *Sample answers are provided.*   1. before Aunt Betty rings the bell   2. Once you have the pertinent facts   3. he ran into an old friend from high school   4. After you clean up your room   5. she loves to go antiquing   6. the dog begins to howl   7. he patted her shoulder and nodded kindly   8. when the border guard arrives   9. I'll get on my knees and beg   10. we'll have to hope for a quick sale

6·6   *Sample answers are provided.*   1. I'll be in my room until you decide to apologize to me.   2. Once you finish painting the bedroom, we'll be able to start on the bathroom.   3. If you really like the car, I'll make you an offer you can't refuse.   4. We'll take the children to the park before it gets too dark.   5. Jim will never play football again unless he has an operation on his knee.   6. John will wash the car while Ruth cuts the grass.   7. When you arrive from the airport, I'll put the kettle on and make some tea.   8. After the movie is over, we'll order a taxi and go the Tom's party.   9. You will be welcome in our home as long as you continue to help out cleaning the house.   10. Once the cake is out of the oven, we can set the table and get ready for the party.

6·7   *Sample answers are provided.*   1. Tom was lounging under a tree; meanwhile, the other boys were loading rocks onto the truck.   2. The woman stole his watch and ring; moreover, she attempted to take a credit card from his pocket.   3. The operation was a miserable failure; consequently, the poor woman died on the operating table.   4. I was supposed to go to class; instead, I decided to go to the river for a swim.   5. Mr. Helms collects old coins; for example, he has several rare gold pieces from Spain.   6. There will be a test tomorrow; in addition, you'll have a lengthy assignment for over the weekend.   7. The woman didn't understand that it was a crime; moreover, she was probably not in her right mind.   8. Jim drank too much, spent too much, and caroused too much; indeed, he acted like a jackass.   9. You place the chemicals in a beaker; next, you light the Bunsen burner.   10. Don't be afraid to ask him for a loan; after all, he can afford it.

6·8   *Sample answers are provided.*   1. I don't care for Brahms   2. I always liked going to parties with her   3. they huddled in their sleeping bags and waited it out   4. a swift current swept them to shore   5. his fame as a criminal reached as far as Asia   6. The weather has been affected by gas emissions   7. Her claim to ownership is ridiculous   8. they've all begun learning to play the flute   9. he lowered his head and fell asleep   10. you won't be allowed to use the car or stay out late with your friends

6·9   *Sample answers are provided.*   1. We need to get home; besides, I think we overstayed our welcome.   2. It's true you weren't driving the car; nonetheless, you're responsible for paying for the accident.   3. Flu season is about over; still, you should consider getting a flu shot.   4. The boys were here first; consequently, there's no food left. 5. He grabbed his bag and left the house; thus began his adventures in New York City.   6. You can stay in the garden and nap; meanwhile, I'll go into the house and make some lemonade.   7. Put on a warm coat; otherwise, you might catch a cold.   8. The blizzard is getting worse; therefore, we're closing the plant and sending everyone home.   9. Jack has on a velvet jacket; incidentally, I have the same jacket in brown.   10. His hands are trembling, and he has a temperature; moreover, he is sweating profusely.   11. You come to work late every morning; in other words, you have no respect for punctuality and are in danger of losing your job.   12. I've read all his books; in fact, I just picked up his latest at the library.   13. The medicine worked miracles; as a result, the sickly child survived. 14. Remain seated; also, keep your seat belt fastened at all times.   15. I'd like to go into the army; on the other hand, I really like the idea of flying.

6·10   *Sample answers are provided.*   1. Although you have a slight accent, your English is excellent.   2. It was hard work, but it helped me to stay in shape.   3. He was unfaithful, yet I find I still care about him.   4. Unless you get out of bed right now, you're going to miss your bus.   5. Since I first met Loretta, I've thought about no other woman.   6. Tom missed every other class; accordingly, he failed.   7. I'll pay for the piano lessons providing that you practice every day.   8. The Joneses bought a new car; in addition, they're having a garage built.   9. You are either crazy or unaware of how your words have hurt me.   10. She acted as if she didn't recognize me.

7   Pronouns

7·1   *Sample answers are provided.*   1. a. It was annoying, because I really needed them. b. Did you read about them in a local newspaper? c. No, I found their description in a flyer.   2. a. My son saw it from his bedroom window. b. I heard my neighbors speaking of it yesterday. c. Its path of destruction was a mile wide.   3. a. They always begged us for food. b. They just have to be with us constantly. c. Our solution was to leave them in the yard at mealtime.   4. a. My father bought me the airline ticket. b. Do you have time to go with me? c. My hotel reservation is for two people.   5. a. What prevented you from going? b. A man at the party asked about you. c. I suppose it was your brother.   6. a. Lots of other things made him laugh as well. b. As soon as you start telling a joke to him, he starts to giggle. c. His sense of humor is very good.   7. a. Did a doctor see her? b. Yes, he was with her about an hour. c. Her condition isn't good.

7·2   *Sample answers are provided.*   1. which greatly frightened the inhabitants   2. which was a fantastic experience 3. who used to play football at Notre Dame   4. about whom I told you earlier   5. which I found in an old textbook   6. who looked a lot friendlier   7. that has a powerful battery   8. whom you punched   9. who waited on me earlier   10. that Mr. Keller sent you

7·3   *Sample answers are provided.*   1. a. , near which a giant castle stood. b. , which they located an inn in. c. that a stranger directed them to. d. no one had ever heard of before.   2. a. from whom he had received the property. b. , whom he had completely relied upon. c. who he had given a down payment to. d. his wife had told him about. 3. a. , upon which lay a large shaggy dog. b. , which the cat liked to sleep under. c. that she had been looking for. d. her husband was sleeping on.   4. a. about whom so much had been written. b. , whom she yearned for in her dreams. c. that she had been interested in since grade school. d. Jane had told her about.   5. a. at which smokers are allowed. b. , which people just argue and complain in. c. that only members can participate in. d. you can learn as much from in a memo.

7·4   *Sample answers are provided.*   1. a. I'll come by for a visit this weekend. b. This is hard to tolerate.   2. a. That restaurant is quite good. b. That is the last straw!   3. a. Are these CDs yours? b. These belong to my cousin. 4. a. Those steaks were delicious. b. Those made me sick to my stomach.

7·5   *Sample answers are provided.*   1. a. In the spring she refreshed herself with a daily walk. b. Why did she buy herself another ring?   2. a. You rarely groom yourself properly. b. You soon gave yourself another reward for the job you had done.   3. a. At dinner we had to serve ourselves. b. We ordered ourselves a large, sweet dessert. 4. a. I angrily reproached myself for those terrible words. b. I pretended to tell myself a similar story.   5. a. They fed themselves on tasty sandwiches. b. They gave themselves wine and snacks and forgot about their guests. 6. a. Tom was interested only in his grandfather. b. Tom was interested only in himself.   7. a. Did you think about the wounded soldier? b. Did you think about yourselves?   8. a. At this moment I thought about the poor flight attendant. b. At this moment I thought about myself.   9. a. Ms. Brown was talking to the young dancer. b. Ms. Brown was talking to herself.   10. a. John and Laura arranged a party for their guests. b. John and Laura arranged a party for themselves.

7·6   *Sample answers are provided.*   1. Much was said, but there was little action.   2. Is either of these cars still for sale?   3. Each is allowed only one piece of luggage.   4. Neither of the girls won a prize.   5. One is a friend of mine; the other is a complete stranger.   6. Everybody loves Raymond.   7. No one understands why they're arguing.   8. Few of them have any knowledge on the subject.   9. Many still believe that global warming is a myth.   10. Each of the contestants has to sing a song.

7·7   1. William himself tried to free the car from the muddy rut.   2. Several of the men themselves heard the strange sounds in the attic.   3. I myself longed to return to my homeland.   4. Ms. Thomas and I ourselves were rather good dancers.   5. The administration itself is responsible for our improved economy.   6. Nancy herself broke down in tears upon hearing the news.   7. You yourself (yourselves) tried to get some help for them.   8. He himself felt ashamed for what had happened that day.   9. They themselves attempted to exploit the situation.

8   Prepositions

8·1   *Sample answers are provided.*   1. The quality of her penmanship was poor.   2. The employee of the month was Tim himself.   3. The study of mathematics requires a good mind and diligence.   4. Is the name of the baby Brian or Ryan?   5. The fabric of his tuxedo was silk.   6. The color of the carpet isn't at all what I want.
7. The government of the United States has three branches.   8. The members of our team are all amateurs.
9. He never spoke of his wife.   10. The cause of hunger is more than just a lack of food.

8·2   *Sample answers are provided.*   1. a. I received a love letter from Ms. Garcia. b. In addition to Ms. Garcia, there are three others up for the management position.   2. a. There's an old TV antenna on their mobile home. b. There's a tent set up in back of their mobile home.   3. a. What do you know about this critical situation? b. In light of this critical situation, I suggest the king go into hiding.   4. a. I'd like to know what lies beyond the wooden fence. b. We should put up a brick wall in place of the wooden fence.   5. a. There's no one in the classroom. b. The students ran screaming out of the classroom.   6. a. Mr. Jackson fell asleep during their weekly meeting. b. They'll prepare another report prior to their weekly meeting.   7. a. Besides another problem that's developing, we still have to solve pollution. b. We won't know what to do in case of another problem.   8. a. With atomic energy still an option, the energy crisis can be avoided. b. We can develop enough electricity by means of atomic energy.
9. a. I need to study long and hard till final examinations. b. In view of final examinations, I suggest you burn the midnight oil.   10. a. He joined the marines despite his stated goal. b. Everything he says and does is contrary to his stated goal.

8·3   *Sample answers are provided.*   1. their tree house   2. foreign tourists   3. the French doors   4. everyone's assumption   5. a store to dry off   6. the convertible and the SUV   7. cabbage and burned bread   8. the bales of hay in the loft   9. more than five months   10. the pretty girl and smiled

8·4   *Sample answers are provided.*   1. the second floor   2. so many fights   3. my sister and me   4. the recommendations of her boss   5. the airport   6. the table and knocked over the vase   7. the new evidence
8. a densely forested hill.   9. six or seven years   10. the guests realized what had happened.

8·5   *Sample answers are provided.*   1. The bus stop is located on the next corner.   2. I'll see you on Friday.
3. The graduates entered the auditorium with pleased smiles.   4. Dad worked up on the roof.   5. The train pulled in just after noon.   6. We had to come on the bus.

8·6   1. I never had anything to do with them.   2. Did you have a good time there?   3. The twins were seated directly behind them.   4. We can probably meet then.   5. Was that rude remark meant for us?   6. We used to have a lot of fun then.   7. I am completely opposed to it.   8. My aunt and uncle built a small house there.   9. We found a map there.   10. Is this a portrait of her?

8·7   *Sample answers are provided.*   1. The women lounged out on the lawn.   2. There were bottles and cans strewn alongside the road.   3. At sunset hundreds of bats appeared above the forest.   4. Several swans swam leisurely on the lagoon.   5. It's because of you that I'm so worried.   6. No one is prettier than her.   7. Their canoe drifted toward the opposite shore.   8. Hang on to the ledge and don't let go!   9. The new student from Brazil worked harder than anyone else.   10. A large group of men stood in front of it and gaped.

9   Using adjectives

9·1   *Sample answers are provided.*   1. a. busy b. Monday was always a busy day.   2. a. strange b. He made a strange noise and fainted.   3. a. dead b. The dead flowers had been severely frostbitten.   4. a. excellent b. This candidate has excellent credentials.   5. a. old-fashioned b. She wore an old-fashioned dress and a bonnet.   6. a. tired b. She had a tired look on her face.   7. a. happy b. Everyone wished her happy birthday.   8. a. nervous b. The nervous man turned out to be a thief.   9. a. wonderful b. We had a wonderful time in the park.   10. a. sad b. The sad look on her face made me want to cry.

9·2   *Sample answers are provided.*   1. a. The CD player is broken again. b. This is my new CD player. c. When did you buy this CD player?   2. a. Young children shouldn't see this movie. b. Their young children are well behaved.
c. These young children shouldn't be punished.   3. a. A yacht is only for the rich. b. Is your yacht a sailing vessel?
c. Who owns that large yacht?   4. a. The new lobby has to be repainted. b. Our new lobby looks fantastic.
c. I've never been in that new lobby in the Foster Building.   5. a. Where are the new pillows? b. Whose pillows are on the floor? c. These pillows are very soft.   6. a. I spend a lot of time with friends and relatives. b. Her friends and

relatives are very nice. c. I never got to meet those friends and relatives.   7. a. The grammar of this language is difficult. b. Your grammar is quite good. c. I don't understand this grammar and its rules.   8. a. Do you understand the mathematical formula I showed you? b. Whose mathematical formula is this? c. I can't trust this mathematical formula.   9. a. The calendar was a great invention. b. My weekly calendar is up to date. c. This calendar is from four years ago.   10. a. This is an unusual painting. b. His most unusual painting is on the other wall. c. That unusual painting is too strange for my taste.

9·3   *Sample answers are provided.*   1. Each student needs a valid enrollment card.   2. Some residents are going to boycott the meeting.   3. This is his first attempt at driving a car.   4. I dropped by to see the elderly man every third day.   5. Are there eleven players on a football team?   6. There haven't been many complaints today.   7. I'll place very few demands on you.   8. Have you been introduced to our daughter?   9. I tried to get tickets in the fifth row center.   10. You're making too much noise.

9·4   *Sample answers are provided.*   1. a. What wristwatch is from Switzerland? b. A Rolex is from Switzerland.   2. a. What blanket is warmer? b. A woolen blanket is warmer.   3. a. What set of towels will look best in the bathroom? b. The yellow towels will look best in the bathroom.   4. a. What length should these boards be? b. These boards should be two meters long   5. a. Which writing implements are older? b. The quill and inkwell are older.   6. a. Which path is more dangerous? b. The path along the cliff is more dangerous.   7. a. Which breakfast menu do you prefer? b. I prefer the continental breakfast menu.   8. a. Whose passport and visa is that on the desk? b. That passport and visa belong to the man from Honduras.   9. a. Whose Cuban relatives are moving to Maryland? b. Juanita's Cuban relatives are moving to Maryland.   10. a. Whose coin purse is that on the table? b. That's Mrs. Timm's coin purse on the table.

9·5   *Sample answers are provided.*   1. I'm a real fan of Elizabethan literature.   2. That judge had served in the divorce court for years.   3. Where is the Kennedy presidential library located?   4. I'll meet you at the recreation center at two P.M.   5. I lost my chemistry book.   6. The faculty lounge is off-limits to students.   7. The White House press corps met in a conference room.   8. The movie theater was packed.   9. How long is baseball season?   10. I always enjoy a Jack London novel.

9·6   *Sample answers are provided.*   1. to be watered   2. to play   3. to admire   4. to spend   5. to write   6. They have new plans to develop.   7. Is there an easier way to clean up?   8. Ms. Johnson still has several exams to grade.   9. In his case, there is nothing to defend.   10. She is the only woman to be praised so enthusiastically.

10   Using adverbs

10·1   *Sample answers are provided.*   1. The children ran out of the school with joy.   2. The baritone could sing better than the soprano.   3. His brother lounged lazily on the sofa and watched TV.   4. Michael showed them his new car with great pride.   5. She acted responsibly after arriving at the accident site.   6. The woman muttered weakly that she was ill.   7. The professor congratulated the students on their progress with a bit of sarcasm.   8. The eight-year-old pianist played the piece beautifully.   9. Little James recited the poem capably and took a bow.   10. Ellen slapped the man and screamed with rage.

10·2   *Sample answers are provided.*   1. a. During the storm, the puppy huddled under the bed. b. The puppy huddled under the bed during the storm.   2. a. Yesterday, Tina found a wallet. b. Tina found a wallet yesterday.   3. a. On the weekend, I usually go hiking. b. I usually go hiking on the weekend.   4. a. Soon I'll be able to play the guitar. b. I'll be able to play the guitar soon. *or* I'll soon be able to play the guitar.   5. a. Next Friday, we're going to a soccer match. b. We're going to a soccer match next Friday.   6. a. In time, Maria became a physician. b. Maria became a physician in time.   7. a. After Paul gets here, we can play cards. b. We can play cards after Paul gets here.   8. a. In June, they were finally married. b. They were finally married in June.   9. a. Last year, I took a course at the college. b. I took a course at the college last year.   10. a. Before I studied English, I didn't understand a word anyone said. b. I didn't understand a word anyone said before I studied English.

10·3   *Sample answers are provided.*   1. We always supported our troops fighting overseas.   2. Larry sometimes had to work on the weekend.   3. I never planned to take art courses at the college.   4. Do you often work at the new plant in the suburbs?   5. Martin always renews his subscription to this magazine.   6. We usually drink coffee with breakfast.   7. Did your parents always live in Europe?   8. My sister and I often baked a cake or cookies.   9. Jim and Ellen seldom went to a dance.   10. Have you never thought of becoming a doctor?

10·4   *Sample answers are provided.*   1. George was in a highly emotional state.   2. What you suggest is totally irrelevant.   3. I feel I can recommend you highly to my manager.   4. Mr. Jones spoke immensely proudly of his gifted daughter.   5. The weekend sale was hugely successful.   6. The women wept profoundly.   7. You behaved really stubbornly.   8. You have a really stubborn nature   9. These claims are entirely false.   10. Your statement is only partially true.

10·5   *Sample answers are provided.*   1. a. I studied there for an hour. b. A stork was nesting on the roof.   2. a. They played outside in the cold. b. They bought the house next door.   3. a. We sat anywhere there was a free seat. b. The portrait hung over the mantle.   4. a. Why did you sleep upstairs? b. The mouse had a home in a small box.   5. a. The miners worked underground for ten hours. b. A strange man lived beyond the river in the hills.   6. a. I think the museum is somewhere in that direction. b. The girls spread out a blanket under a leafy tree.

10·6   1. a. Surely, you don't believe his story. b. You surely don't believe his story.   2. a. Undoubtedly, the man is a genius. b. The man undoubtedly is a genius.   3. a. Personally, I feel I can place my trust in this woman. b. I personally feel I can place my trust in this woman.   4. a. Presumably, Mr. Lee has a wonderful new job in Boston. b. Mr. Lee presumably has a wonderful new job in Boston.   5. a. Cleverly, Daniel found a seat next to the pretty girl from Korea. b. Daniel cleverly found a seat next to the pretty girl from Korea.

10·7   *Sample answers are provided.*   1. Clearly, they usually don't care what anyone thinks.   2. Foolishly, he left on a hike last week during a storm.   3. Bravely, they entered the very gloomy cemetery.   4. Fortunately, I sometimes have a brief moment of brilliance.   5. Personally, I think you're a really nice person.   6. a. I quickly ran to the window and saw Bill. b. Fortunately, I ran to the window and saw Bill. c. I ran to the window and suddenly saw Bill. 7. a. Wisely, Juanita destroyed the strange object. b. Juanita immediately destroyed the strange object. c. Juanita destroyed the very strange object.   8. a. After she fainted, they carried her into the living room. b. They carefully carried her into the living room. c. They carried her into the living room around five o'clock.   9. a. Presumably, the old men sat around the little table. b. The extremely old men sat around the little table. c. The old men sat silently around the little table.   10. a. Her left leg is seriously broken. b. Her left leg is once again broken. c. Her left leg is broken in two places.

11   Present and past participles

11·1   *Sample answers are provided.*   1. Laughing   2. dining   3. ticking   4. shocking   5. fighting   6. Living in Denmark   7. sailing   8. Billowing   9. leaving   10. spreading

11·2   *Sample answers are provided.*   1. Shredded   2. Having heard the hooting of an owl   3. Stunned by her words 4. burned   5. stained   6. located   7. Startled by the noise   8. watched   9. left   10. found

11·3   *Sample answers are provided.*   1. a. This is our new writing table. b. The written word can be powerful.   2. a. The sound of breaking glass frightened her. b. A broken nose is a serious matter.   3. a. A charging bull is nothing to joke about. b. The man charged was a member of a gang.   4. a. A leaking pipe is a sign of trouble. b. Any leaked information is a danger.   5. Lying under a tree, Newton spied an apple swaying above him.   6. Hoping for better weather, the tourist stared out into the foggy street.   7. Driving at a hundred miles an hour, the sickly man nearly had an accident.   8. Placed front and center on the dresser, the trophy was John's prized possession   9. Beaten by two bullies, the little boy wiped his face and ran home.   10. Driven to madness, the queen fell across her throne in tears.

11·4   *Sample answers are provided.*   1. lazily   2. swiftly   3. badly   4. precariously   5. proudly   6. finely 7. carefully   8. against the door   9. thoroughly   10. beautifully

11·5   *Sample answers are provided.*   1. Jim felt fully rested.   2. The parents listened to their happy daughter giggling. 3. Merrily strumming on an old banjo, the farm boy closed his eyes and sang.   4. Having been voted president, Ellen came up to the microphone to speak.   5. The room was filled with his treasures collected over the years. 6. The topic suggested by a professor was of no interest to them.   7. The lawyer challenged the witness sputtering nervously.   8. Driven to madness, the king ran naked through the castle.   9. Having to remain at home, the feverish girl curled up in bed and wept.   10. The sound of the vigorously bubbling soup made the hungry boy smile.

12   Using infinitives

12·1   *Sample answers are provided.*   1. the food for fifty guests   2. a fine university   3. during Professor Williams's lecture   4. in the symphony   5. a hero   6. under the stars   7. as a member of Congress   8. a plan for success   9. to the top of Pikes Peak   10. a simple poem

12·2   *Sample answers are provided.*   1. until dark   2. behind a leaning fence   3. the garage door   4. a book on Greek mythology   5. the front hall   6. move the refrigerator   7. to take a vacation   8. to be asleep on the sofa   9. to sell me a used car   10. to turn off your laptop

12·3   *Sample answers are provided.*   1. is part of my family's values   2. will require a lot of money   3. is often a shallow goal   4. requires many skills   5. has many dangers   6. should be a goal of yours   7. will take many decades   8. has always been my wish   9. will make my parents happy   10. is my greatest hope

12·4   *Sample answers are provided.*   1. a. Her desire will never be to marry Jack. b. Such an idea, to marry Jack, will never be accepted by your father. c. It took great courage to marry Jack.   2. a. The young man's desire is to become a famous actor. b. Your reason for quitting school, to become a famous actor, isn't rational. c. It was Bill's obsession to become a famous actor.   3. a. My reason for taking this class is to understand grammar better. b. Your commitment, to understand grammar better, is one that more students should make. c. It is no easy thing to understand grammar better.   4. a. His dream had become to run in the marathon. b. This notion, to run in the marathon, was a joke. c. It's a wonderful idea to run in the marathon.   5. a. She hoped not to become conceited. b. His warning, not to become conceited, went unheard. c. It is in the realm of possibility not to become conceited. 6. a. The boy's wish is never to cry. b. The idea, never to cry in public, is absurd for a child. c. It seemed impossible never to cry.   7. a. To develop great skill playing the guitar was his only desire. b. Her goal, to develop great skill playing the guitar, is just a pipe dream. c. It was difficult to develop great skill playing the guitar.

12·5 *Sample answers are provided.*   1. to show his discontent   2. to be certified   3. to lend a hand   4. to contact regarding your application   5. to open the gates   6. to spend the night   7. to avoid rush hour traffic   8. to correct these problems   9. to become a manager   10. to tackle

12·6 *Sample answers are provided.*   1. I want nothing more than to enjoy the music and relax.   2. My wish is to be supported by people like you.   3. She came here to locate her missing daughter.   4. The woman to applaud is our former director.   5. To be contradicted in this way is not pleasant.   6. This is a difficult word to spell.   7. To forgive is a virtue.   8. I came to be forgiven for what I've done to you.   9. Is there any way to eliminate such waste?   10. It's not my job to judge you.

12·7 *Sample answers are provided.*   1. a. to answer some e-mails b. to finish her report   2. a. to develop new procedures b. to contact other experts   3. a. To learn to play the flute b. to become team captain   4. a. to hope for another chance b. to wait for help to come   5. a. to surrender b. to seek other advice

13 Using gerunds

13·1 *Sample answers are provided.*   1. a. Borrowing some money could solve our problems. b. Our only recourse was borrowing some money.   2. a. Is collecting stamps your hobby? b. My passion is collecting stamps.
3. a. Traveling around New England would be expensive. b. My suggestion has always been traveling around New England.   4. a. Complaining will get you nowhere. b. His worst habit became complaining.   5. a. Can solving her money problems improve her life? b. Her goal needs to be solving her money problems.   6. a. Swearing is forbidden! b. There will be no swearing.   7. a. Jogging in the park is nice on a good day. b. My favorite thing isn't jogging in the park.   8. a. Being on the team is a privilege. b. His only source of pride is being on the team.
9. a. Crying from sadness is human. b. The boy's weakness wasn't just crying.   10. a. Avoiding an accident must be every driver's goal. b. My reason for driving like this is avoiding an accident.

13·2 *Sample answers are provided.*   1. a. I thought about washing the car. b. I thought about not washing the car.
2. a. Do you like vacationing in Florida? b. Do you like not vacationing in Florida?   3. a. Visiting Uncle Charlie is a bad idea. b. Not visiting Uncle Charlie is a bad idea.   4. a. I prefer getting up at dawn. b. I prefer not getting up at dawn.   5. a. Spending the weekend at the cabin was a great idea. b. Not spending the weekend at the cabin was a great idea.   6. a. Having a wholesome breakfast was rare in their family. b. Not having a wholesome breakfast was rare in their family.

13·3 *Sample answers are provided.*   1. a. We've been hiking for six hours. b. I've never really enjoyed hiking.
2. a. Professor Jones isn't requiring another essay this term. b. Requiring typed note cards is unfair.
3. a. Are you suggesting that I help with the dishes? b. I was thinking about suggesting a new approach to this project.   4. a. We'll be employing several new people next week. b. Employing minors is a bad idea.   5. a. The chimps are imitating us. b. I don't like your imitating my mannerisms.   6. a. The police investigating the crime are from another precinct. b. Investigating procedures have been set up.   7. a. I saw the men training out on the field. b. This training course will help to reduce injuries.

13·4 *Sample answers are provided.*   1. a. I'm tired of being your assistant. b. This promotion, being your assistant, doesn't come with a pay raise.   2. a. We had a blowout from stopping too suddenly. b. Their explanation for the damage, stopping too suddenly, was contradicted by their son   3. a. I can't get used to sunbathing and swimming on this crowded beach. b. His favorite activities, sunbathing and swimming, held no appeal for her.   4. a. The town has no interest in razing the old church. b. The city's decision, razing the old church, cost the congregation a lot of money.   5. a. They caused a fire by playing with matches. b. The dangerous behavior, playing with matches, required a severe punishment.

13·5 *Sample answers are provided.*   1. to travel in Spain / traveling in Spain   2. to say hello to us / saying hello to us
3. to calm down / calming down   4. to babysit / babysitting   5. to draw / drawing   6. to pack a lunch / NA
7. to speak louder / speaking louder   8. to fine the man / fining the man   9. to use such language / using such language   10. to scream at his mother / screaming at his mother

14 Idioms

14·1 1. pulling my leg   2. about   3. well off   4. feel like going   5. a lot of hot air   6. You can bet your bottom dollar   7. You had better not   8. from scratch   9. this red tape   10. a real card

14·2 *Sample answers are provided.*   1. a. Tina mumbled something b. My sister said a rude word   2. a. dancing with me b. helping us clean house   3. a. squander my money b. buy an expensive car   4. a. The answer b. The meaning of the word   5. a. to give birth b. to give him a kiss   6. a. This is a lot of b. I hate having to deal with
7. a. The salesman had b. Because she lied, she had

14·3 *Sample answers are provided.*   1. My family has never been well off.   2. As usual, his bragging is just a lot of hot air.   3. You'll have to count those coins from scratch.   4. There's something fishy about where he said he was last night.   5. The coach has a bone to pick with the captain of the team.   6. Accept the outcome and keep a stiff upper lip.   7. Marie doesn't feel like playing chess tonight.   8. Once again Tim found himself in hot water. 9. We better find some shelter from this storm.   10. Because of his drinking, his business went to the dogs.

14·4   1. at all   2. really   3. should have   4. mind   5. Well   6. by the way   7. or so   8. How about 9. really   10. at all

14·5 *Sample answers are provided.*   1. a. This is a really thrilling novel. b. I really never met you before.   2. a. Would you mind if I smoked? b. I don't mind his bad habits.   3. a. I'm not mad at all. b. Tina's not at all interested in Jake. 4. a. I should have listened to my mother. b. You shouldn't have said that.   5. a. I weigh 150 pounds or so. b. We could use two hundred dollars or so.   6. a. His career in music went to the dogs. b. His business went to the dogs because of his gambling.   7. a. By the way, my mother is coming for a visit. b. By the way, I plan to be at Jack's party, too.   8. a. How about buying this CD? b. How about lending me a few dollars?   9. a. Well, that's the silliest thing I ever heard. b. Well, are you finally dressed?   10. a. Do you feel like watching some TV? b. Mom didn't feel like going for a walk with us.

15   Short responses and interjections

15·1 *Sample answers are provided.*   1. Naturally.   2. Don't mention it.   3. For heaven's sake.   4. I have no idea. 5. Of course.   6. What a pity.   7. Terrific!   8. Not at all.   9. Apparently.   10. Unfortunately, not.

15·2 *Sample answers are provided.*   1. He made the girl in the box disappear.   2. Are you available to help with our move?   3. She did something to the engine, and the car started right up.   4. None of the kittens survived. 5. I'm on the sofa trying to take a nap.   6. Do you enjoy German opera?   7. I have so many bills that I can't go on the trip.   8. Will your sister be joining us for dinner?   9. Each member of the winning team will receive a trophy.   10. I think that Jane is putting on weight again.

15·3 *Sample answers are provided.*   1. Great   2. Ah   3. Good   4. Bravo   5. Ouch   6. Hurrah   7. See 8. So   9. Well   10. No

15·4 *Sample answers are provided.*   1. Now, place a worm on the hook and you're ready to fish.   2. Ah, I love sitting in a nice hot tub of water.   3. Great! Now I have to do all the work by myself.   4. See! I told you that their dog bites!   5. There, don't you feel better now?   6. Well, that's a story I'll remember for the rest of my life. 7. Why, I never knew you could play the violin.   8. Here, let me show you how that's done more efficiently. 9. So, this young woman thinks she can be a ballerina.   10. The situation has, indeed, shown some improvement.

16   Antonyms and contrasts

16·1 *Sample answers are provided.*   1. Math is easy for me, but I find grammar difficult.   2. Is the glass half empty or half full?   3. Bill found his wallet but lost his keys.   4. I often go to the opera but seldom enjoy myself. 5. You may be right, but I'm not entirely wrong.   6. I'll send you a receipt after I receive your check.   7. Tim is smart but acts stupid.   8. Don't start something you can't finish.   9. The kitchen floor isn't dry yet but still wet. 10. The young people try to help the old.

16·2 *Sample answers are provided.*   1. All are assembled for the meeting, but none are prepared to vote.   2. Tina always claimed she told the truth, but she never told anything but lies.   3. Life is as beautiful in his new homeland as it was ugly in his war-torn country.   4. There is nothing you said before this incident and nothing you said after it that can make a difference.   5. Although the view below was wonderful, flying so high above the earth made Jim nervous.   6. He is as different from his brother as black is from white.   7. Dark colors make her look businesslike, but dressed in light colors, she looks young and radiant.   8. By day, Mary seems plain, but at night she puts on her most seductive dress and makeup and leads the life of a vamp.   9. The corrupt politician had dirty hands, and nothing he could do would make them clean again.   10. Phillip believed the hour was still early, but it was late and he woke his wife from a sound sleep.

16·3 *Sample answers are provided.*   1. , only tragedy and an outlook on life that is sad   2. and ended at a long, straight highway that led back to the city   3. , yet she knew that he had meant only to be kind   4. nor encourage you to travel to such a dangerous place   5. but soon realized it was the single figure of a man and his shadow 6. and would not be sober for weeks to come   7. ; however, his behavior when speaking to women was clumsy 8. despite his claim that he was innocent of the affair   9. , but my grandmother knows they're real 10. , but their defeat meant the end to the war

16·4 *Sample answers are provided.*   1. The farmers harvested the scarce crop of wheat   2. Although he pretended his outburst was accidental   3. How can you advance in your career   4. I will not condemn this woman 5. The enemy will seem to surrender   6. Although he had been honored on the battlefield   7. She had been fertile and born seven children   8. Despite years of discord   9. The tone of his voice was mild   10. Although my heart may seem fragile

16·5 *Sample answers are provided.*   1. he carelessly dropped a flask on the floor   2. He had a cheerful smile   3. that a hopeless situation could be remedied   4. I spent a very restless night   5. for a stranger was helping with her thankless job   6. some people are mindless of other people's feelings   7. Because the situation seemed so helpless   8. Although there was nothing sinful about him   9. Although any aid would have been useful   10. and began the next cheerless task

16·6 *Sample answers are provided.*   1. The boy wasn't bashful; he was just unsure of himself.   2. Although you weren't driving the car, you aren't guiltless in this matter.   3. We're grateful for your patience in this matter.   4. He was drunk and lay almost lifeless on the ground.   5. The young boxer was knocked senseless.   6. He looked into the dark corner and saw a shapeless image.   7. Tim couldn't believe his ears and was speechless.   8. A long life of disappointments had made her spiteful and bitter.   9. His words were timeless and will be quoted for centuries.   10. The homeless man struggled to stay warm.

16·7 *Sample answers are provided.*   1. Although he seemed so bright, there was something ignoble about his character.   2. Although the pups and kittens got along, there seemed something unnatural about their relationship.   3. Although he explained it again, the class still misunderstood his words.   4. Although the investigation was thorough, the crime remained unsolved.   5. Although his father warned that there would be consequences, Johnny continued to misbehave.   6. We don't want you to become discouraged from achieving your goals.   7. My intent was to please you, not to dissatisfy you.   8. The two veterans both suffer from a severe disability.   9. Their lawyer was well known for his displeasing manner.   10. I'm afraid that this line of clothing has been discontinued.

17 The passive voice and the subjunctive mood

17·1   1. a. She learned several new songs. b. Several new songs were learned by her.   2. a. The bartender is pouring two beers. b. Two beers are being poured by the bartender.   3. a. Andrea has borrowed our new SUV. b. Our new SUV has been borrowed by Andrea.   4. a. We will never catch that huge fish. b. That huge fish will never be caught by us.   5. a. Jack was carefully photographing the scene of the accident. b. The scene of the accident was being carefully photographed by Jack.   6. a. I usually lead the band. b. The band is usually led by me.   7. a. The farmer had plowed the field by late afternoon. b. The field had been plowed by the farmer by late afternoon.   8. a. The pianist was playing the sonata without error. b. The sonata was being played without error by the pianist.

17·2   1. Oranges and lemons are grown in this region of California.   2. The thief has already been identified.   3. Her portrait is being painted as a surprise for her husband.   4. He will be greeted enthusiastically.   5. The old car was repaired and repainted.   6. Despite the inconsistencies, his story was believed.   7. Ms. Lopez has been recommended for the job.   8. The evidence was being examined in preparation for the trial.   9. His strange behavior has been noted in the final report.   10. Was he recognized?

17·3 *Sample answers are provided.*   1. It is being reported that there was a terrible accident on Highway 11.   2. Has it been stated that those courses will not be offered?   3. It was quietly remarked that the new boss doesn't know what he's doing.   4. It was proved that the epidemic was finally under control.   5. It is written that each person should be responsible for his or her own actions.   6. It was announced that the contract was awarded to a foreign company.   7. It is estimated that more than 50 percent of the citizens are against new taxes.   8. It has been decided to send you to boarding school.   9. It was mentioned that several delegates wanted to vote against him.   10. It has been argued that no progress has been made in the negotiations yet.

17·4   1. a. A counterfeit check was sent to him by the woman. b. He was sent a counterfeit check by the woman.   2. a. A tie and shirt will be lent to the man by me. b. The man will be lent a shirt and tie by me.   3. a. A crate of oranges is being shipped to us by Aunt Mary. b. We are being shipped a crate of oranges by Aunt Mary.   4. a. Was a medal being awarded to them by the judges? b. Were all of them being awarded a medal by the judges?   5. a. Two new houses have been shown to the young couple by the broker. b. The young couple has been shown two new houses by the broker.

17·5   1. Robert must be rushed to the hospital.   2. Someone has to be held responsible for any act of vandalism.   3. I should not have been found guilty.   4. These men will want to be paid fairly.   5. The other teams can't be instructed by professionals.   6. The roof must have been struck by lightning.   7. No one was able to be rescued.   8. This student had wanted to be admitted to the university.   9. The diplomats ought to be greeted by the head of state.   10. Grandfather has had to be operated on.

17·6 *Sample answers are provided.*   1. a. Your reputation will be ruined by such behavior. b. My new skirt is ruined!   2. a. The town hall had been destroyed by a massive fire. b. His confidence was destroyed.   3. a. The garage is being painted by two college boys. b. The living room is painted and looks great.   4. a. The same word had been misspelled by the boy several times. b. The last word in this sentence is misspelled.   5. a. The patient could not be healed with ordinary medicines. b. Your wound is finally healed.

17·7 *Sample answers are provided.*   1. this plan be rejected   2. give up all her rights   3. remain a matter for the court   4. a committee be formed to look into the situation   5. be changed for your personal needs

Sample answers are provided.   1. If only we found a solution to the problem.   2. If only it weren't true.
3. If only Jim were able to return home for a while.   4. If only the sign weren't seen by so many people.
5. If only I had driven a little faster.   6. If Sarah brought home a pizza, the kids would eat nothing else.
7. If you would permit me to sit with you for a while, I would love to chat about your travels.   8. If you had insisted on my staying longer, I would not have left so early.   9. She would have to agree with you if she understood your motives.   10. I would be grateful if you were a bit kinder to my sister.

18 Phrasal verbs

18·1 *Sample answers are provided.*   1. a. I'll be out until suppertime. b. I was out with Tina last night.   2. a. That handsome guy is really with it. b. Buy some new clothes and get with it.   3. a. The man in the red jacket seems to be up to something. b. Those kids are up to no good again.   4. a. Uncle Jake broke down and cried. b. I saw tears in her eyes and knew she was breaking down.   5. a. The comedian broke up the audience. b. I have to break up with you.   6. a. We breezed through lunch and hurried back to work. b. Anna breezes through every test.
7. a. You can count on me for about twenty dollars. b. Don't count on Hal for any help.

18·2 *Sample answers are provided.*   1. on his brother   2. in unannounced   3. up this conversation   4. this story
5. on her husband   6. with the lawn mower   7. away during the night   8. the problem   9. with a skirt and blouse   10. at

18·3 1. to lay off   2. let on   3. has something against   4. to make of   5. made up with   6. made up
7. make up   8. letting on   9. lay off of   10. lead / on

18·4 *Sample answers are provided.*   1. She tried to pass off the piece of glass as a gem.   2. Someone set off the fire alarm!   3. It's time we set off for home.   4. What do these symbols stand for?   5. I was wrong. I take back what I said.   6. You ought to take up knitting.   7. At six I walked out into the evening air and hurried home.
8. You can't just walk out on me.   9. I'll never warm up to your mother.   10. Did you water down this coffee?

18·5 *Sample answers are provided.*   1. a. Tom broke down her silence. b. Tom broke her silence down. c. Tom broke it down.   2. a. I'll follow up the story. b. I'll follow the story up. c. I'll follow it up.   3. a. They laid off our department. b. They laid our department off. c. They laid us off.   4. a. He's just leading on the girl. b. He's just leading the girl on. c. He's just leading her on.   5. a. We let down Dad. b. We let Dad down. c. We let him down.
6. a. He passed off the watch as a Rolex. b. He passed the watch off as a Rolex. c. He passed it off as a Rolex.
7. a. They set off a firecracker. b. They set a firecracker off. c. They set it off.   8. a. I'll warm up the coffee. b. I'll warm the coffee up. c. I'll warm it up.   9. a. Don't water down my martini. b. Don't water my martini down.
c. Don't water it down.   10. a. The beautician made up her face. b. The beautician made her face up. c. The beautician made it up.

18·6 1. out on   2. off as   3. in   4. down   5. away   6. off   7. up to   8. up   9. up for   10. with

19 Letter writing and e-mail

19·1 1. Henry Higgins
1556 W. Palmer Street, Apt. 3
Dallas, TX 75211

2. Ms. Margaret Rutherford
32 Fifth Street
Tucson, AZ 85701

3. Mr. Ben Roberts
3103 N. Scott Street, Third Floor
Boston, MA 02197

19·2 *A sample letter is provided.*

August 30, 2009

Dear Mary,

It was good to see you again last week. I'm glad to hear that your mother is well again and able to go back to work.

I'm happy to say that I'm back at work, too. I found a job in Peoria teaching eighth-grade math in Mather Junior High School. I'm so happy about this position, and I can hardly wait for the kids to show up next week. It's been a lot preparation, but I'm enjoying everything.

Gayle and I are having a housewarming party on Labor Day. We hope you can come to Peoria and help us celebrate. We've got the guest room ready for your visit.

We're eager to see you again.

Fondly,

Mark

19·3   1. Ms. Alice French, Chief Accountant
Design Department
The Stone Company
3103 Scott Street
Denver, CO 80211

Re: A Proposal for the Jenner Project

Dear Ms. French:

2. Mr. Charles Gibbs, Manager
Kaufman Brothers Shoes
1515 S. Wellington Avenue
Atlanta, GA 30303

Dear Mr. Gibbs:

19·4   *A sample letter is provided.*

June 19, 2009
1416 Miller Road
Washington, DC 20099

Mr. Victor Wallace
Sunnyside Travel Agency
909 E. Culver Avenue
St. Petersburg, FL 33705

Re: Travel to Florida

Dear Mr. Wallace:

I received your brochures last week and am interested in a little more information regarding a ten-day vacation in one of two Florida resorts: Sunny Sands in Sanibel and Beacon House on Key Largo. My preferred arrival dates are either Saturday, September 12, or Saturday, September 19.

We are a family of five. Our three children range in age from four to eleven years, and we worry that the resorts that interest us are oriented only to adults. Are there activities for young children? Are there babysitting services? Naturally, the cost for a vacation like this is a concern. Your brochure did not specify how many guests can stay in one room. If our children can be in a single room with us, that would make this vacation more affordable.

Do some of the rooms provide kitchenettes? Does the resort have a laundry for guests? Are there tennis courts and a gym?

If a Florida resort vacation will cost too much, I would consider taking my family on a Caribbean cruise during the same time frame in September. Please send me information on such cruises only if the cost of the Florida resort is more than $190.00 per night for our family of five.

Thank you.

Sincerely,

Henry Smythe

Henry Smythe

19·5   *A sample e-mail is provided.*

To: Mike Towers (mike@datafirm.net)

From: James Hill (jimhill@datafirm.net)

Subject: Did you forget?

Mike,

I lent you my surfboard more than a month ago, and you still haven't returned it. I know you've been back from Hawaii for more than a week and can't be using it here in Minneapolis's snow. Just kidding. But I need it by next week. My brother wants to use it.

Don't forget about the party at Laura's house on Saturday. Are you bringing a date? I asked Kim to go with me, but she said she has other plans. Know another girl who needs a date?

See you soon.

Jim

19·6   *A sample e-mail is provided.*

To: Jean King (jeanking@datafirm.net)

From: Marie McDonald (mm800@datafirm.net)

Subject: My application

Dear Ms. King:

I enjoyed our conversation over the phone on May 2. I was very pleased to receive your invitation to send you my application for employment with Datafirm and my résumé. I feel certain that you must have received them well over a week ago, and I am eager to learn what you think. Since last speaking with you, I have completed my course on the Italian renaissance and received a grade of A. That means that my course work is now ended, and I shall receive my degree in June, which would be just in time to start with Datafirm. Looking forward to your reply.

Sincerely,

Marie S. McDonald

19·7 *A sample e-mail is provided.*

To: L. L. Jenkins (jenkins@datafirm.net)

From: Robert Smith (bobsmith@datafirm.net)

Subject: Invoice number 5544

Dear Sir or Madam:

On October 5 of this year, I signed a contract with your company to paint my living room and dining room. The work began two weeks late and took five days instead of two. However, it is not the time the job took but the quality of the work that I am contacting you about. The two coats of paint I contracted for turned out to be just one coat, and the old paint is showing through.

I'd like someone to come out to complete the job to my satisfaction, or I will feel compelled not to send you my final payment as shown in Invoice #5544. Please contact me immediately to resolve this problem. Thank you.

My phone number: (312) 555-6061

Robert Smith, Attorney at Law

19·8 *A sample text message is provided.*

Hi, Tom. Check out Keller's Café on Main Street. It's terrific. If U like it, we can get dates and meet there Saturday. C U 2nite at the meeting. Gene

20 Let's write!

20·1 *Sample answers are provided.* 1. His girlfriend has been waiting for a gift from him since her birthday last month. 2. A customs official was fired for being drunk and coming late to work. 3. When I was in Washington, D.C., I had a brief interview with a representative from Colorado. 4. Whenever I travel abroad, I try to speak the language of the country I'm visiting. 5. Who said that the defendant is found guilty and will have to pay a fine? 6. Although Germany is located near Denmark, it is not a Scandanavian country. 7. His former wife was not ugly, but his new girlfriend is quite beautiful. 8. A week ago the barn burned down because it had been struck by lightning. 9. The weak infant is still struggling to regain his health after being born with an infection. 10. He has been behaving as if he had won first prize.

20·2 *Sample answers are provided.* 1. a peace treaty still has not been negotiated 2. about two months ago and are eagerly waiting for the concert 3. that silly movie and not about the problem of global warming 4. but when she got an answering machine, she hung up 5. our trying to save a little money 6. and as fast as possible hurry over to Jane's house 7. what a funny costume 8. We really still love each other 9. is it that she had a terrible accident 10. printed the first Bible on an invention that would change the world

20·3 *Sample answers are provided.* 1. A house in the suburbs is / a condo in New York 2. The blade of his sword was / than the farmer's ax 3. I suspect that my frog will / than the fat one you brought 4. A watch such as this is / is still an interesting keepsake 5. you have been dishonest / I am unable to understand how you got so much money 6. Which road is / to the Canadian border 7. The shy girl was / to run for school president 8. use this tool to get that bolt off 9. Have they finally / do they need more time 10. am discouraged / encouraged by your actions

20·4 *Sample sentences for your paragraph are provided.* The new wing of our house was constructed during the spring of 2008. My grandmother, whose bedroom is conveniently located on the first floor, has arthritis. The fireplace I told you about in my last letter still isn't working.

20·5 *Sample sentences for your paragraph are provided.* I probably ought to tell you about Mr. Burns, who was my favorite high school teacher. I had to drop out of track due to an injury during the mile run. Jim Taylor was dating my ex-girlfriend until she and I got together again last month.

20·6 *Sample sentences for your paragraph are provided.* By tomorrow I'll have read every article he ever wrote. He suggested we be prepared for a rise in oil prices sometime next quarter. The managers tried to pass off the misleading numbers as an accounting error.

20·7 *Sample sentences for your paragraph are provided.* Our family lived in a small apartment in the city, but when I was ten, we moved to a house in the suburbs. I entered my first college class as if I were full of confidence and knew what I was doing. The wedding ceremony was supposed to be performed by both a minister and a rabbi.

21 Progress check

21·1
1. d 2. a 3. a 4. c 5. b 6. d 7. c 8. a 9. c 10. b 11. d 12. a 13. a 14. d 15. b 16. b
17. d 18. c 19. c 20. b 21. d 22. a 23. d 24. c 25. b

21·2
1. a 2. c 3. a 4. b 5. b 6. a 7. a 8. a 9. a 10. a 11. c 12. d 13. d 14. b 15. a 16. b
17. a 18. b 19. a 20. d 21. c 22. a 23. b 24. b 25. b

21·3
1. a 2. d 3. a 4. b 5. b 6. d 7. c 8. a 9. d 10. a 11. c 12. b 13. a 14. d 15. c 16. d
17. a 18. c 19. b 20. d 21. a 22. d 23. b 24. b 25. d